Downhill Xenomorphs

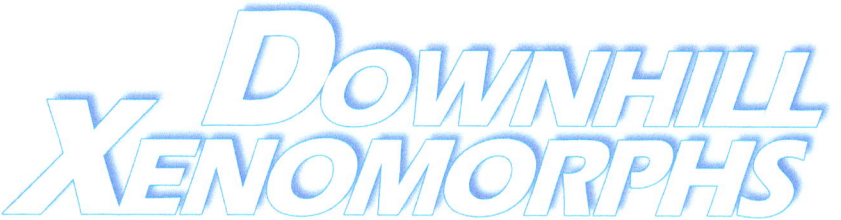

First published by PWCA, LLC 2023

Copyright © 2023 by Jonathan Galimore

ISBN: 9798397469180

Imprint: Independently published

All rights reserved. No part of this publication may be reproduced, stored or transmitted in any form or by any means, electronic, mechanical, photocopying, recording, scanning, or otherwise without written permission from the publisher. It is illegal to copy this book, post it to a website, or distribute it by any other means without permission.

This novel is entirely a work of fiction. The names, characters and incidents portrayed in it are the work of the author's imagination. Any resemblance to actual persons, living or dead, events or localities is entirely coincidental.

First edition

Prepare to witness a convergence of two vastly different worlds—a collision that few have ever had the privilege to experience. Nestled within the snowy peaks of a secluded mountain range, lies a secret hideaway where an enigmatic species, the Xenomorphs, have found a new habitat. A new home. In this captivating photo book, renowned wildlife photographer, **Jeff Stendhal**, unveils a collection of breathtaking images that blur the boundaries between science fiction and reality.

With unrivaled access granted by a group of intrepid explorers, Stendhal captures the incredible journey of these formidable beings as they navigate the treacherous terrain of an unfamiliar planet. Through his lens, he captures the grace, power, and awe-inspiring beauty of these skiing Xenomorphs as they conquer the slopes, gliding effortlessly through the powdered snow, their elongated limbs adapting seamlessly to the environment.

.5

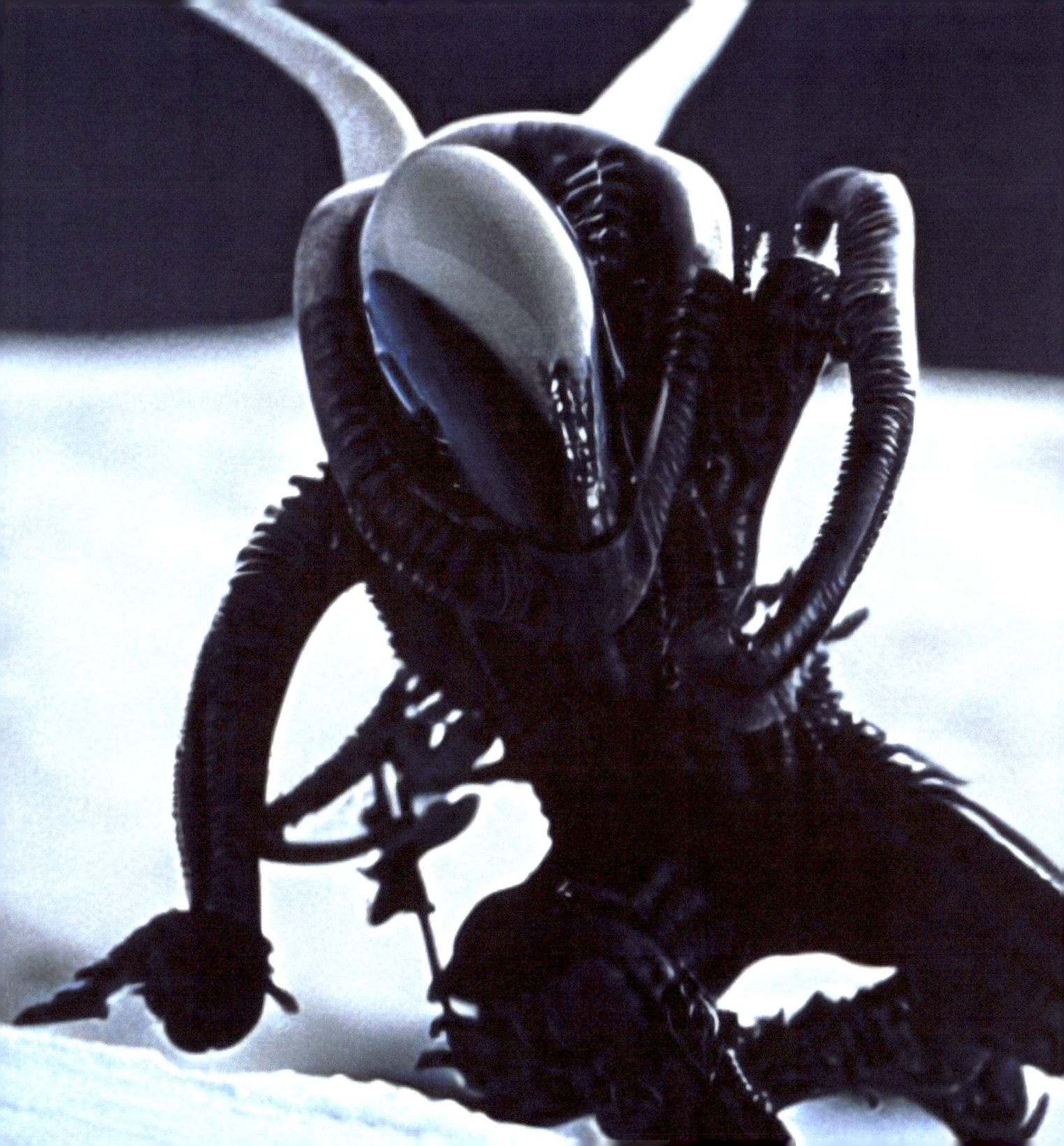

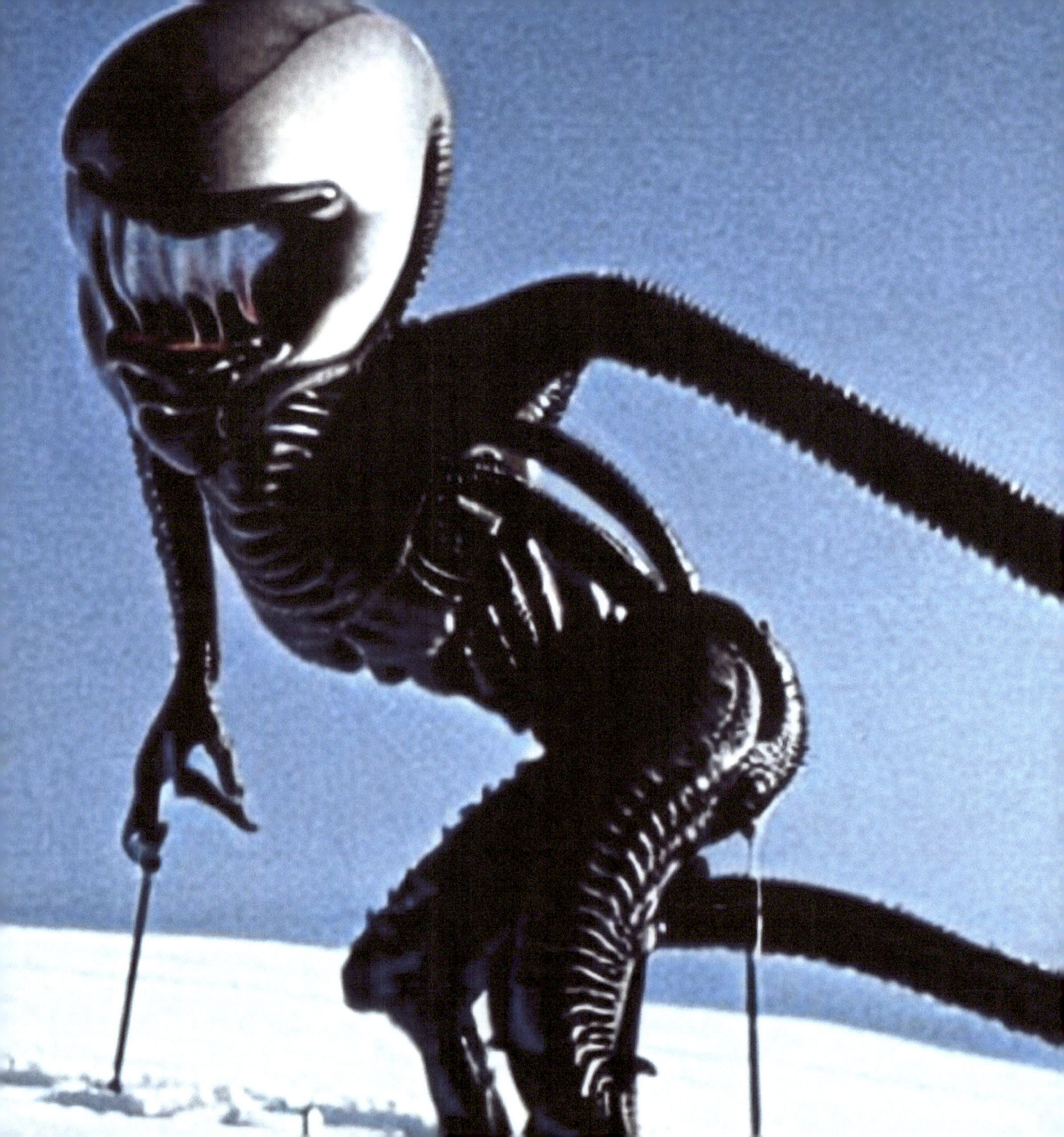

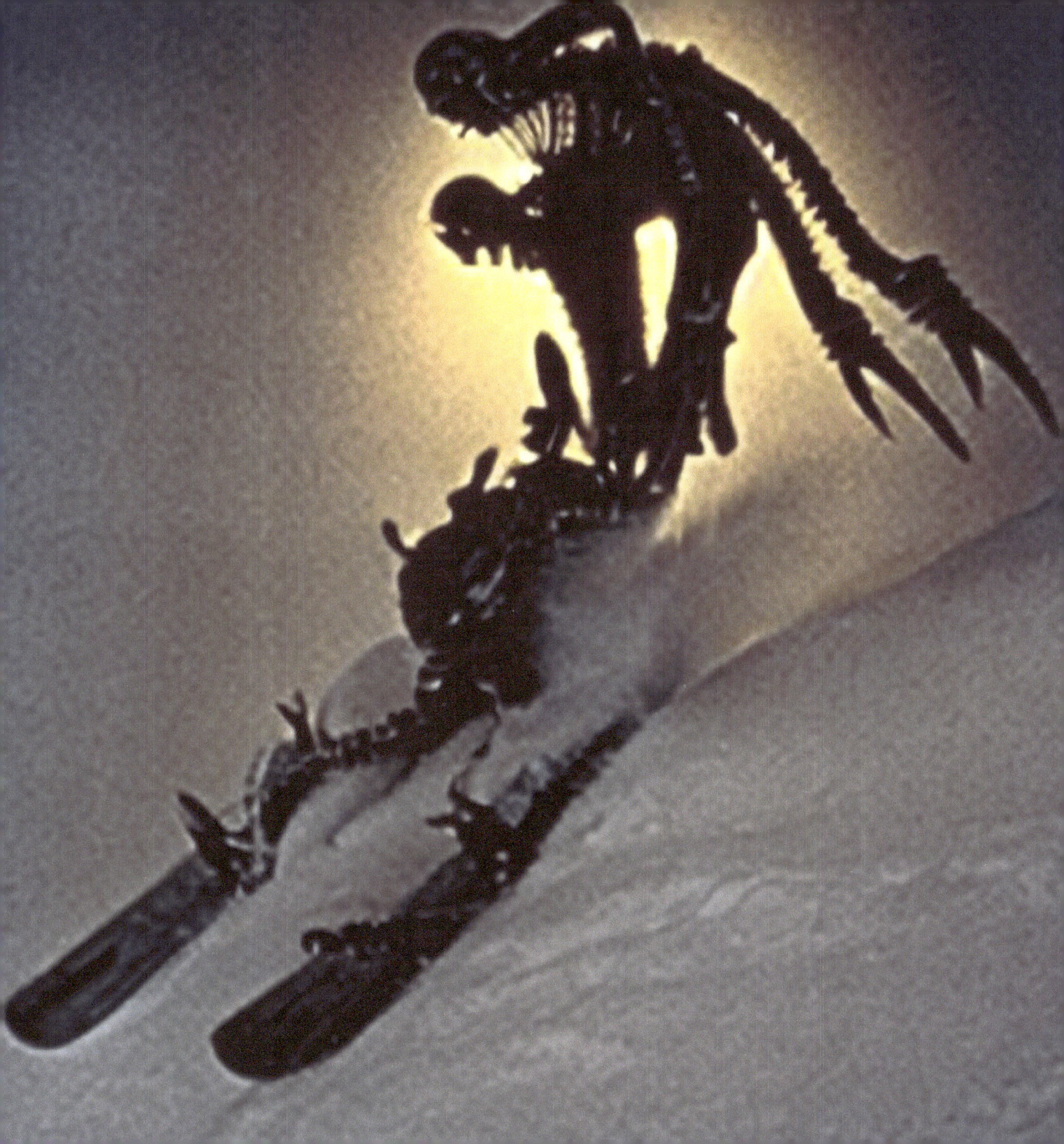

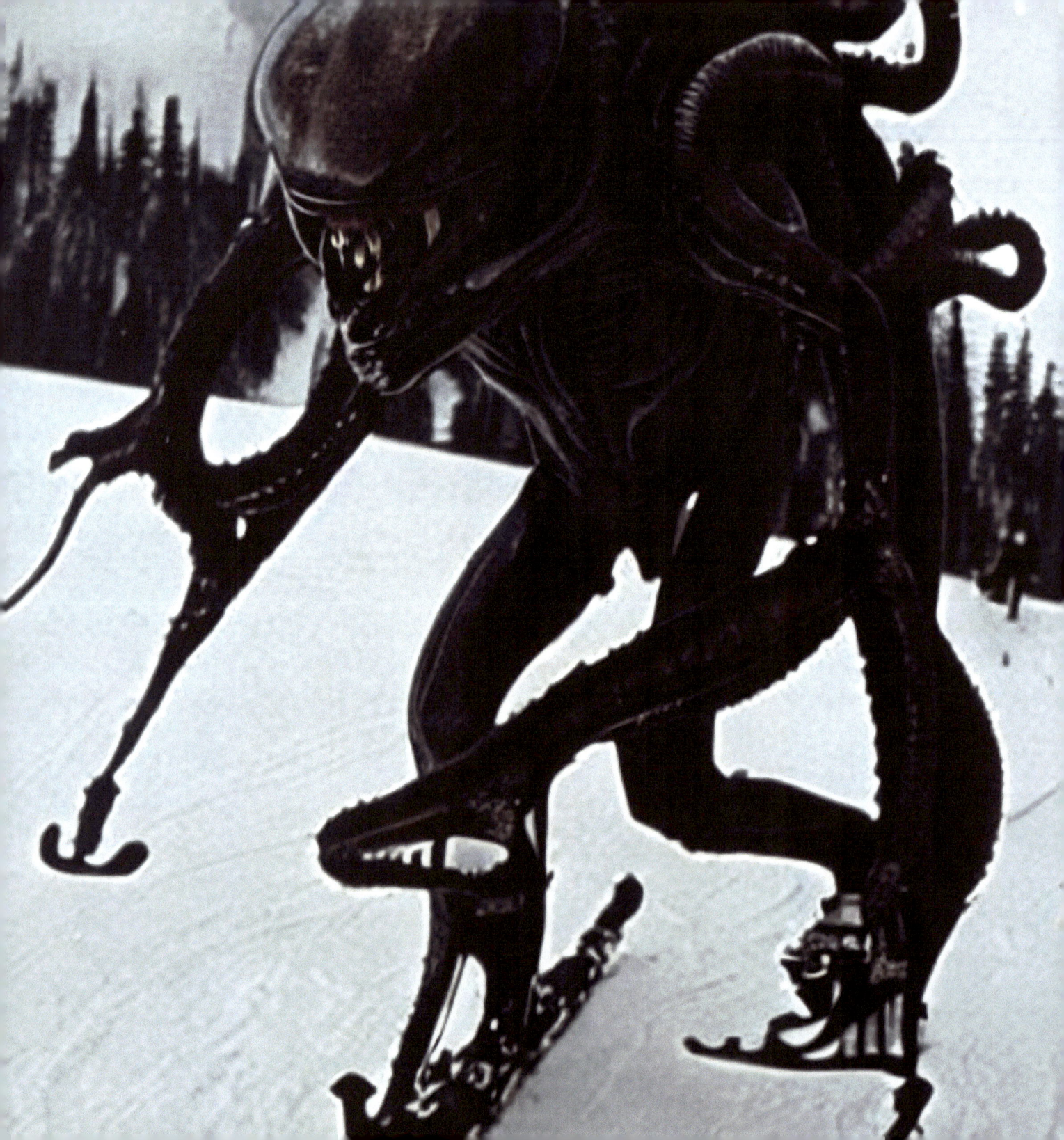

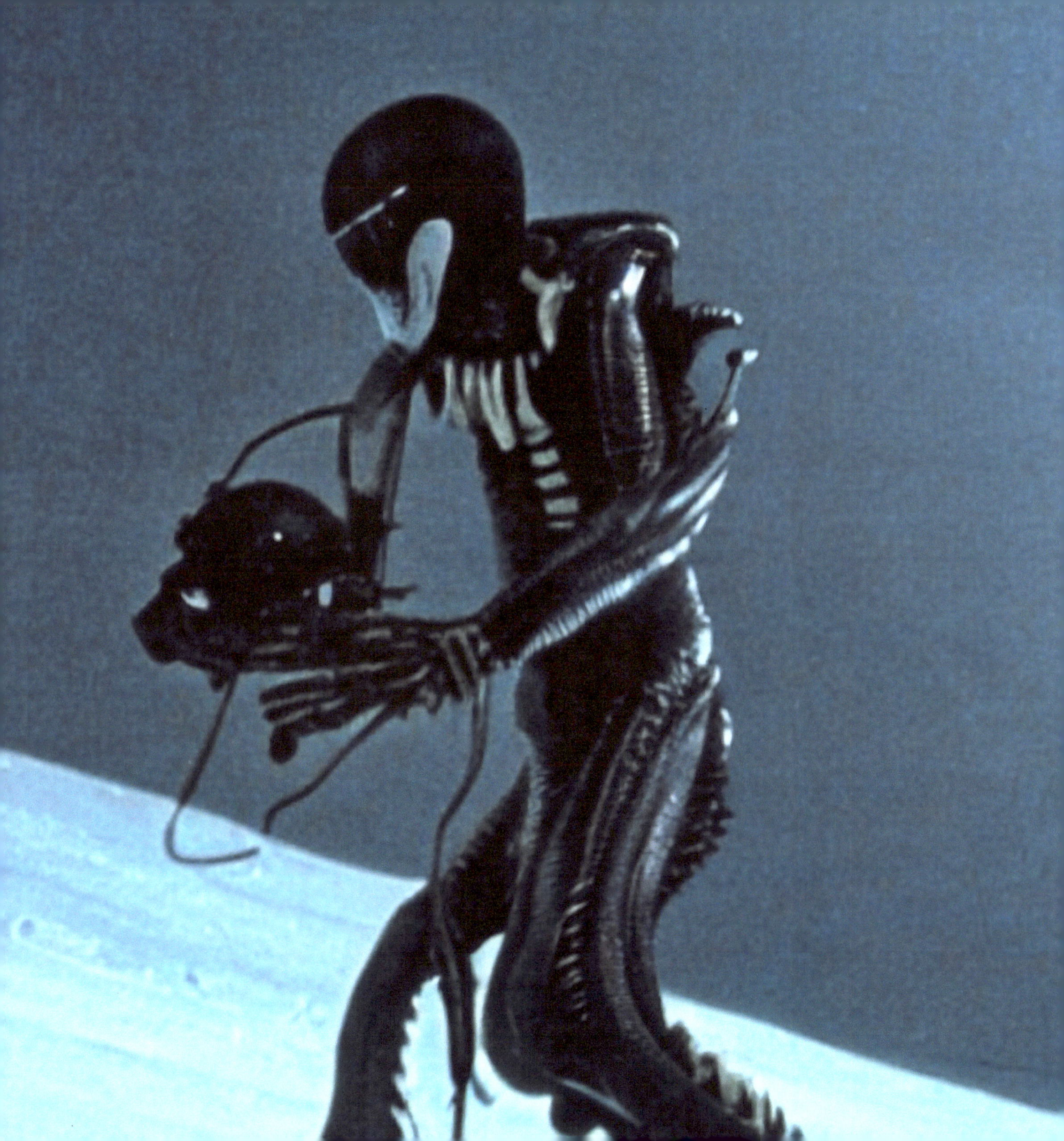

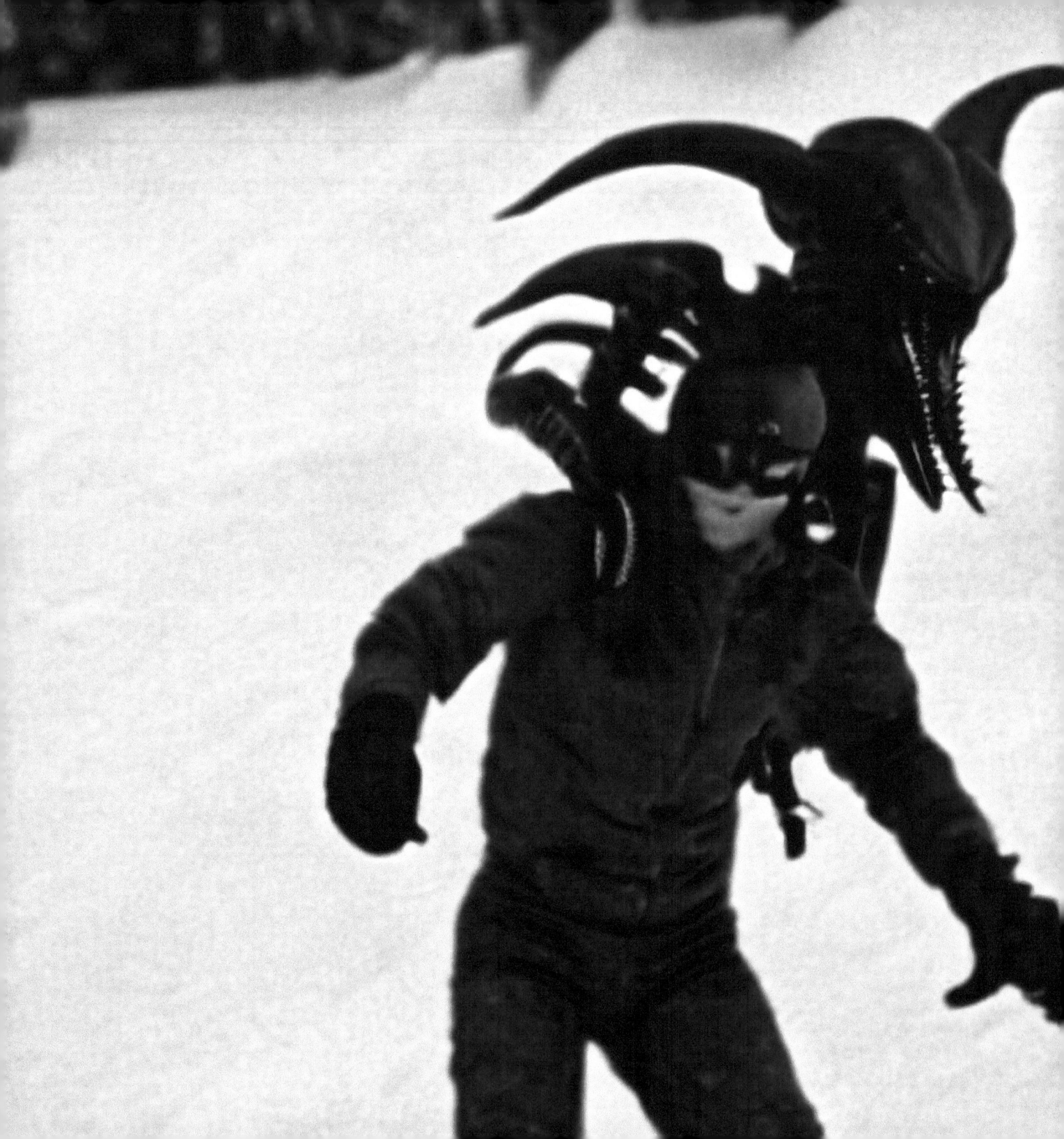

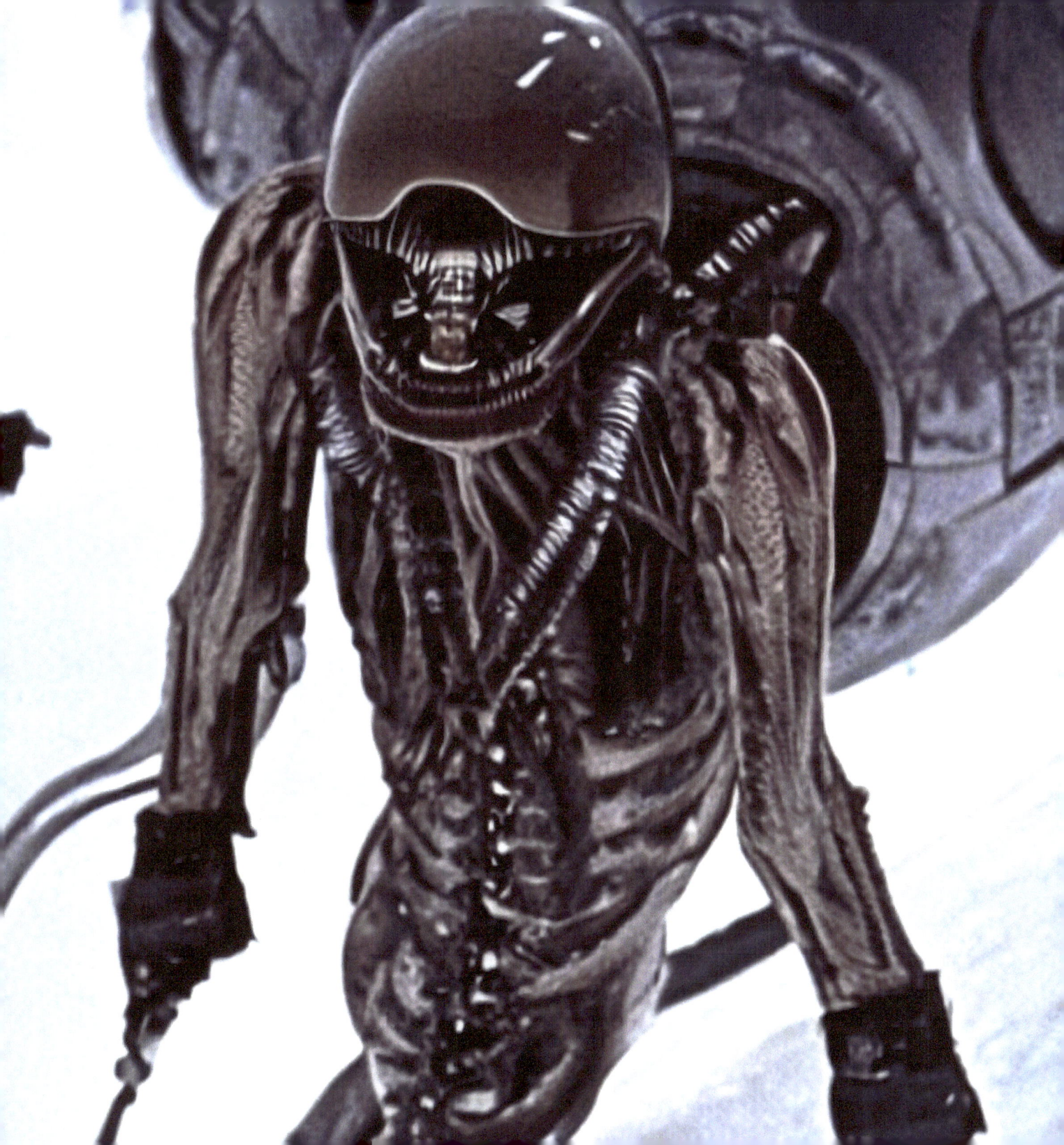

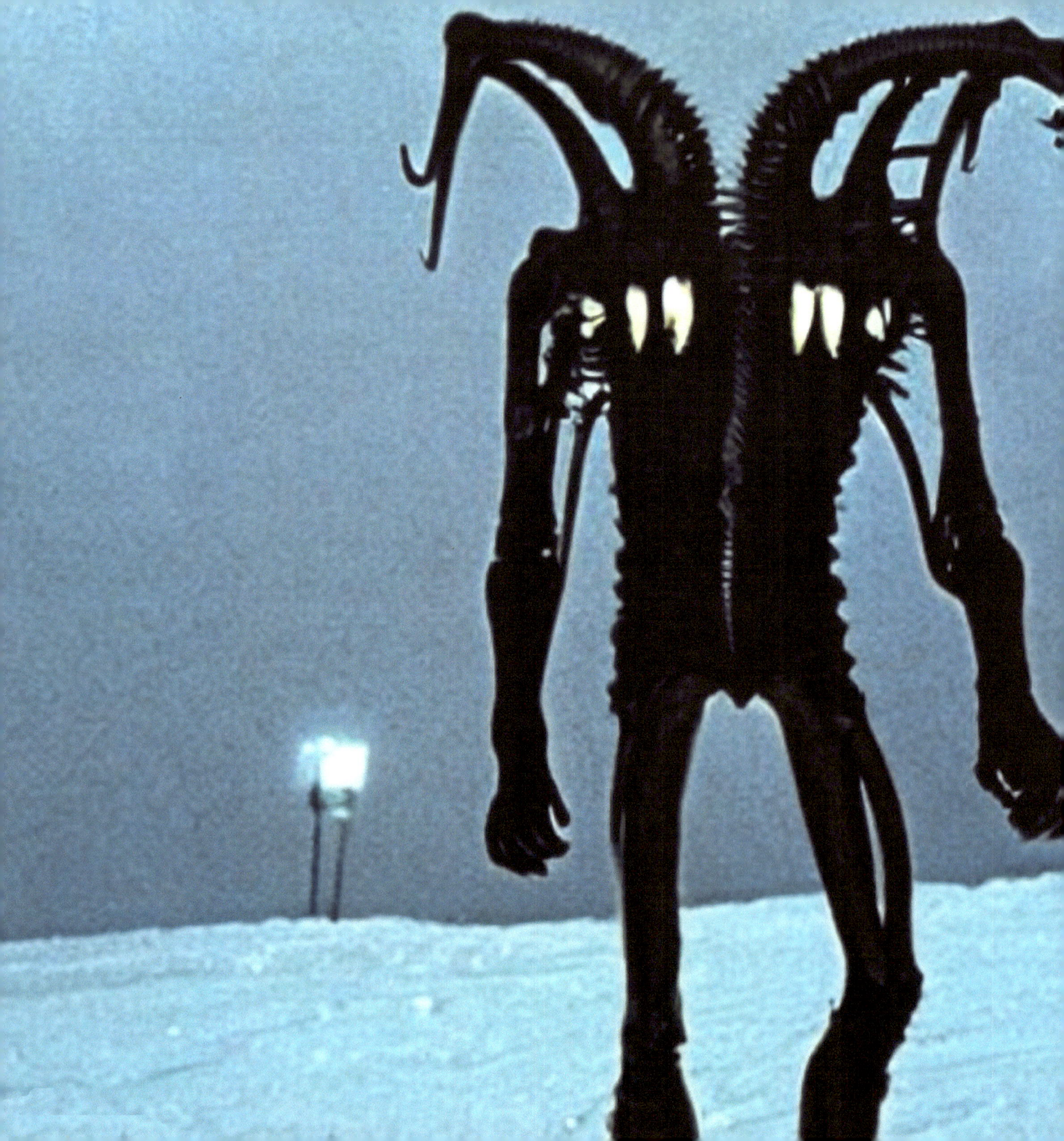

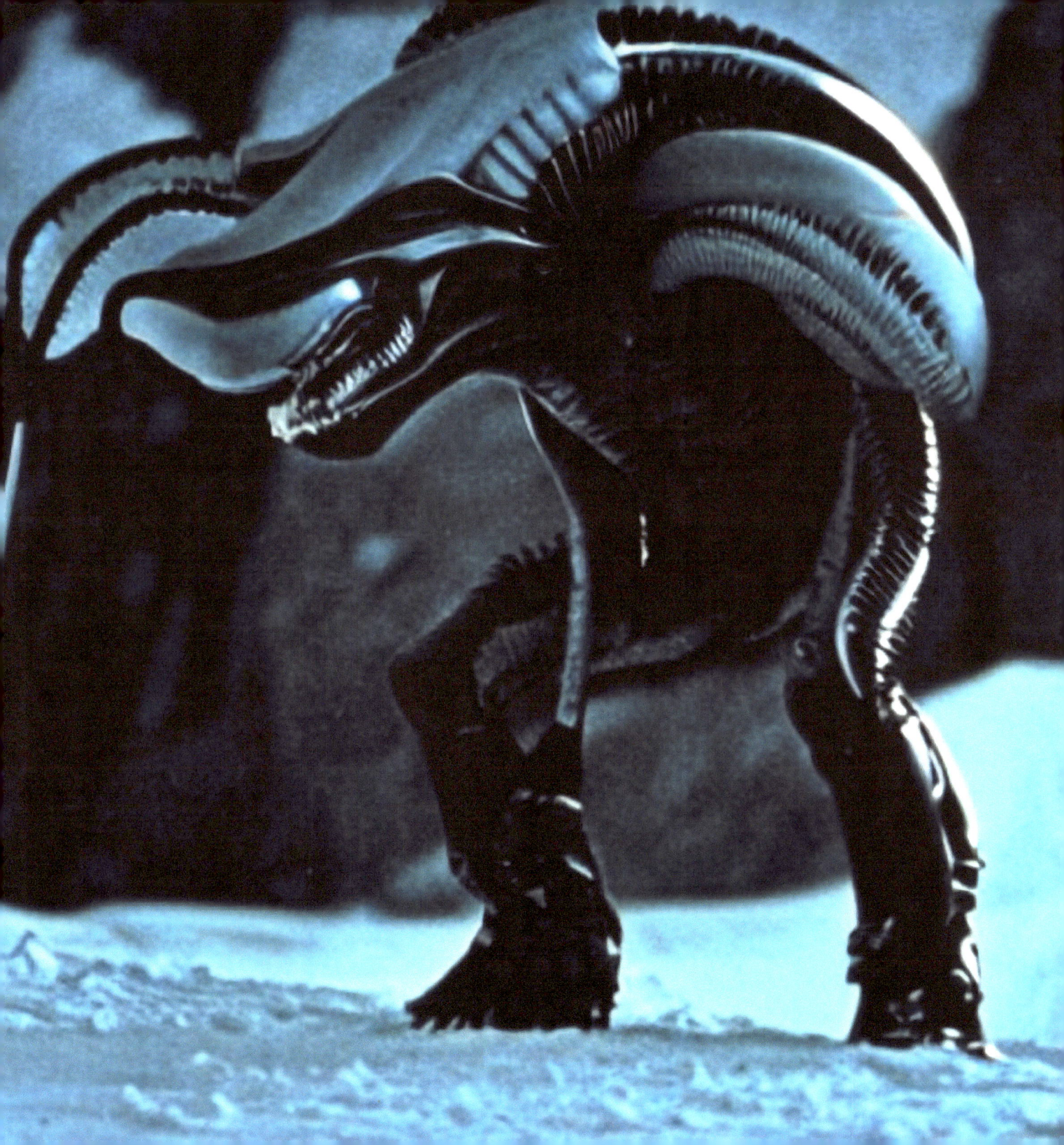

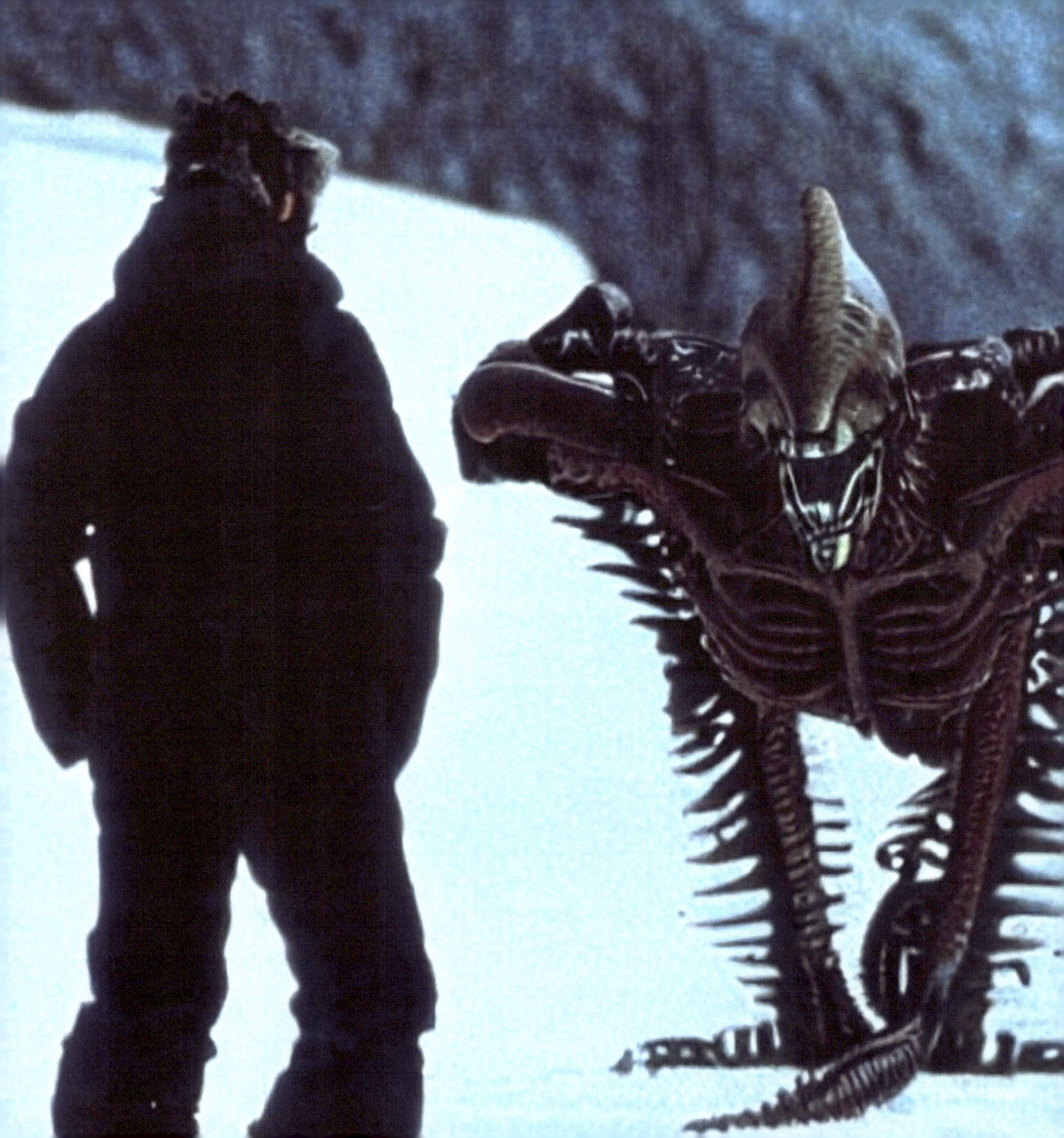

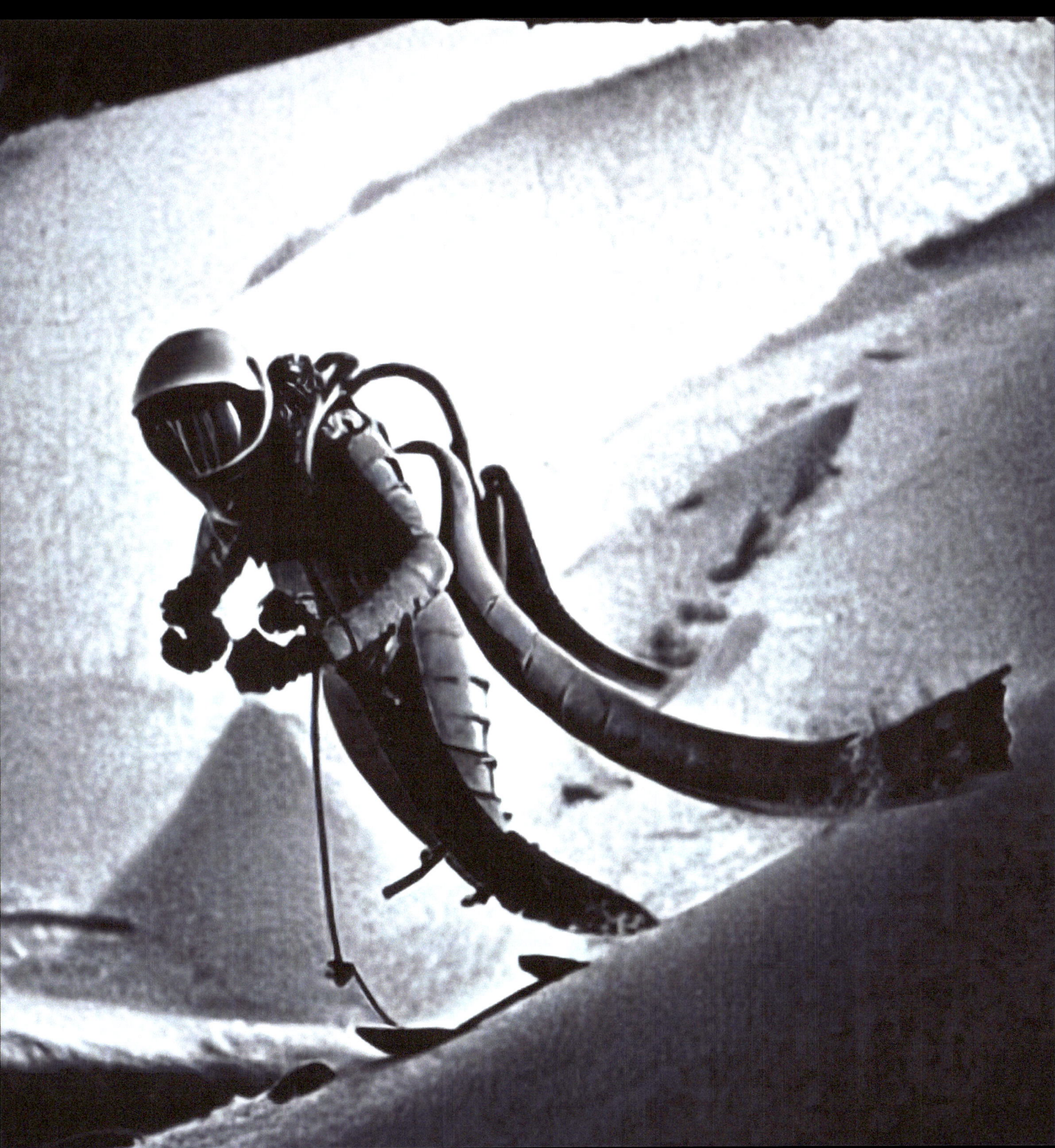

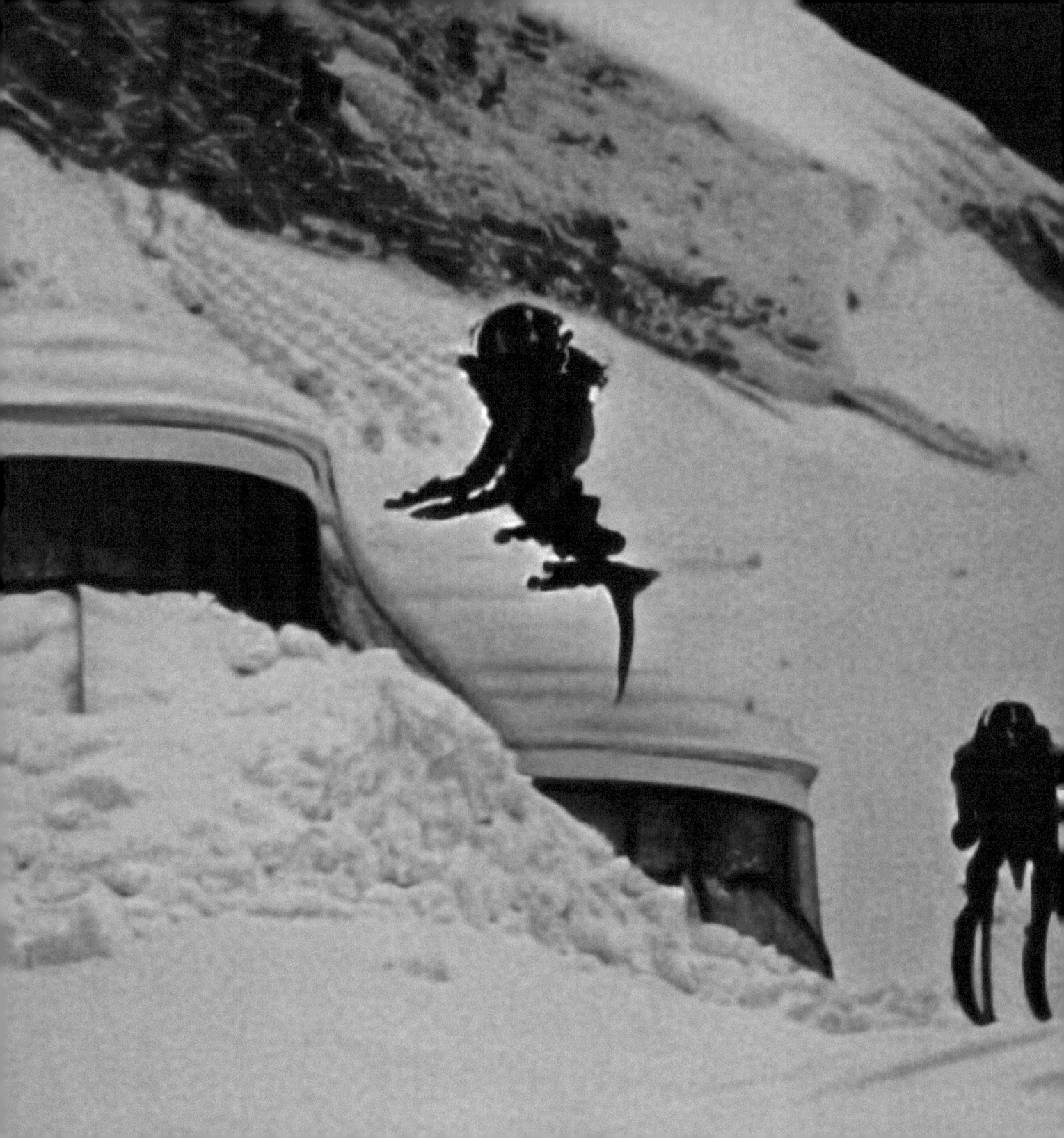

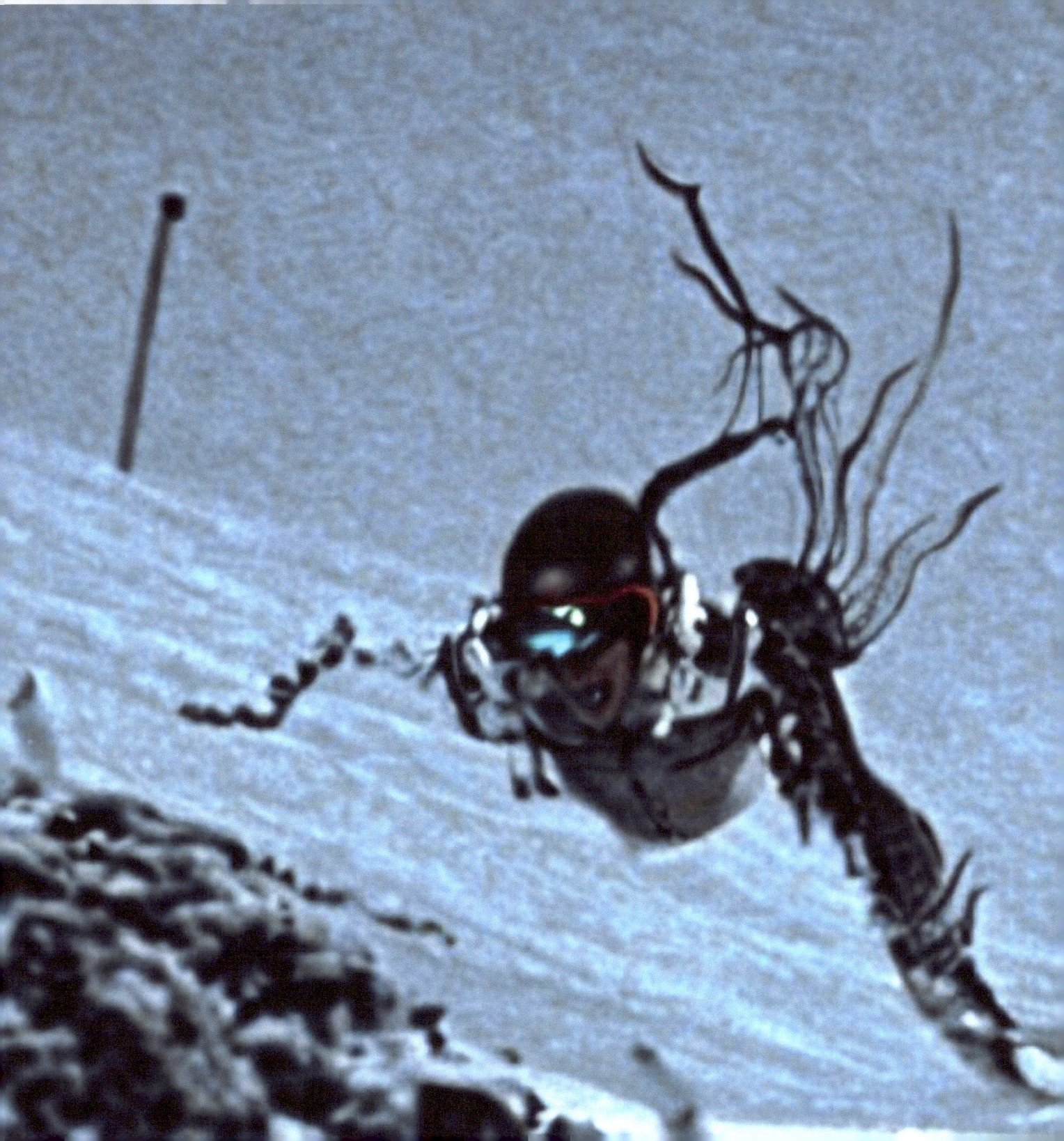

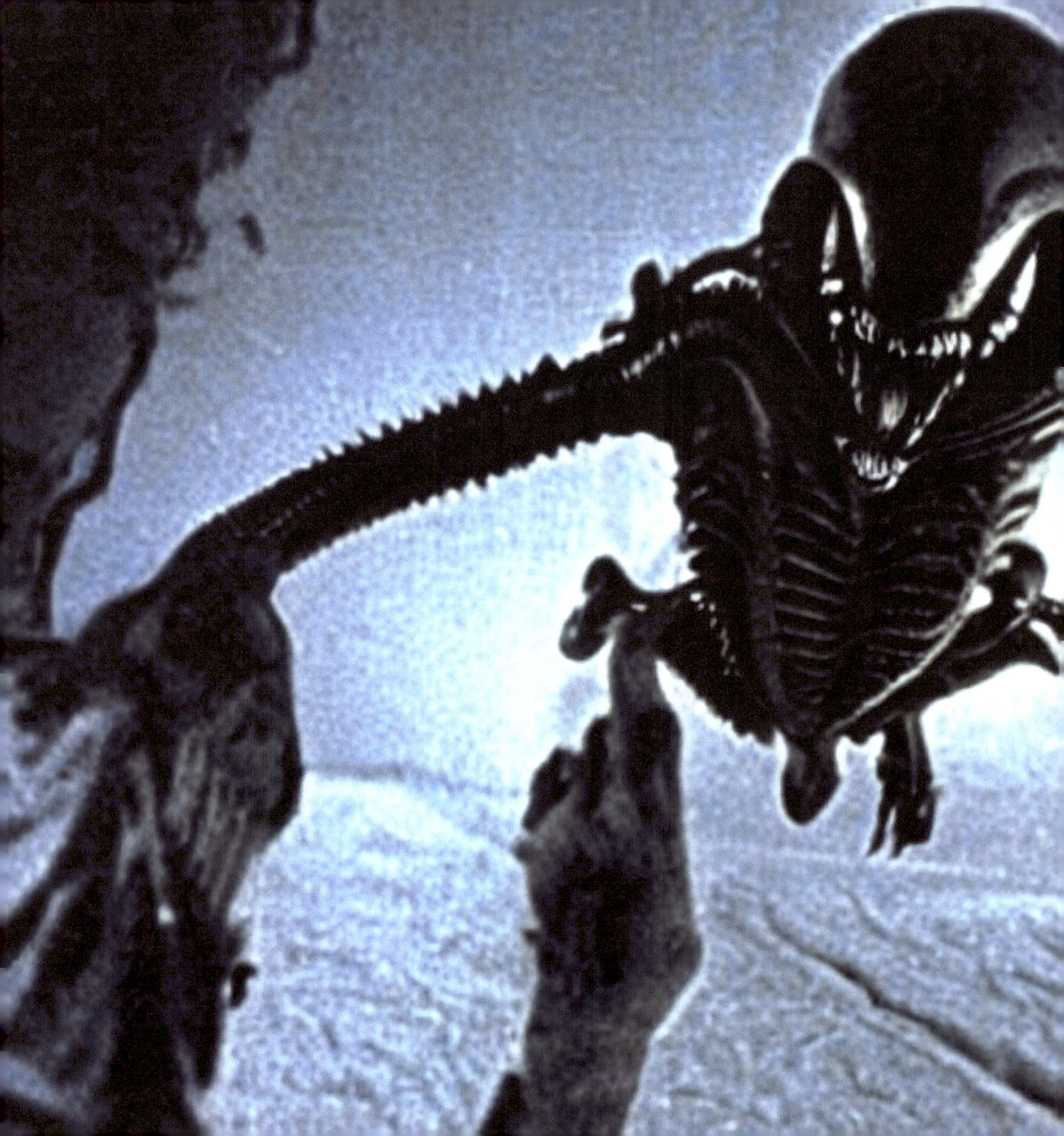

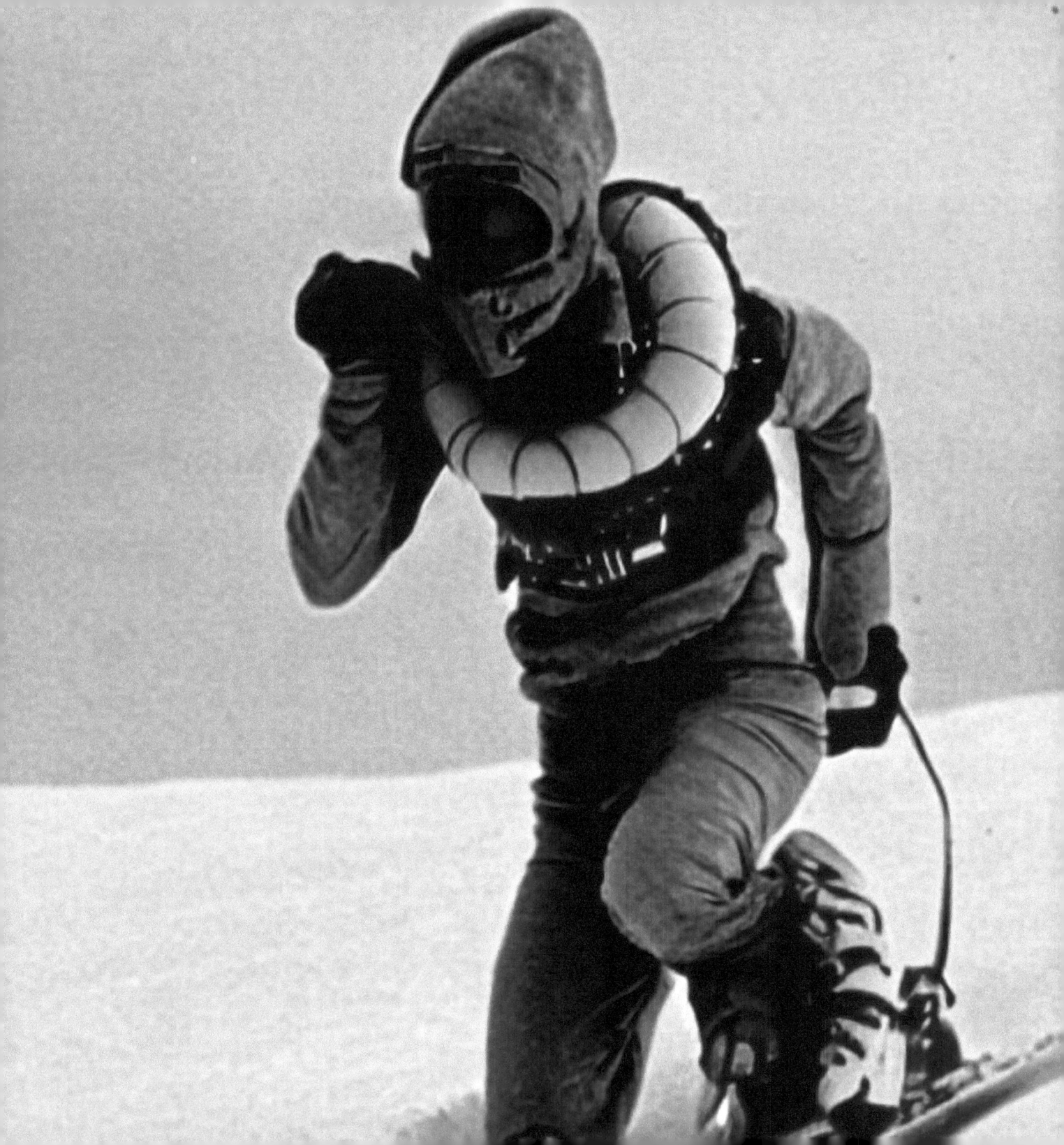

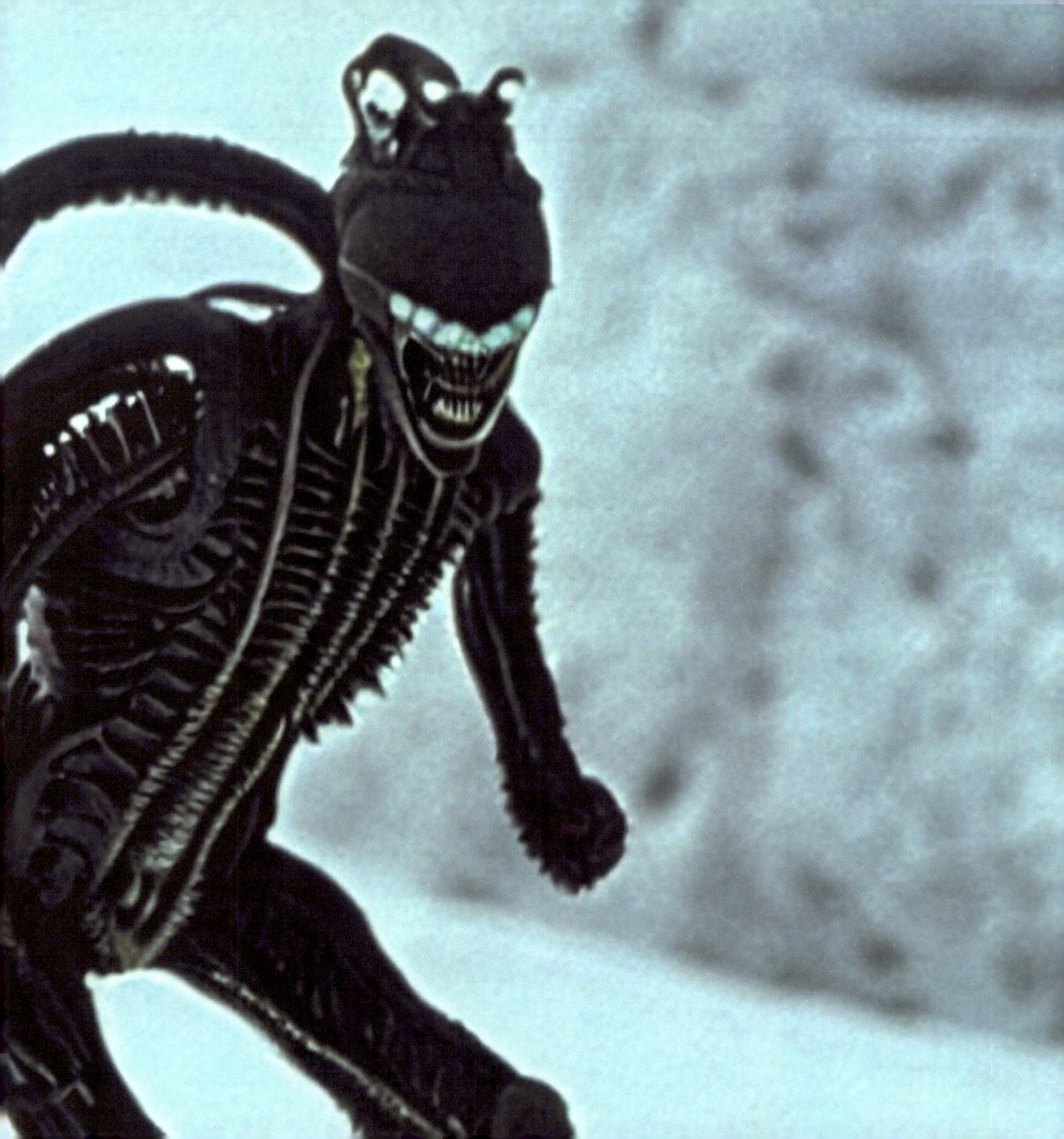

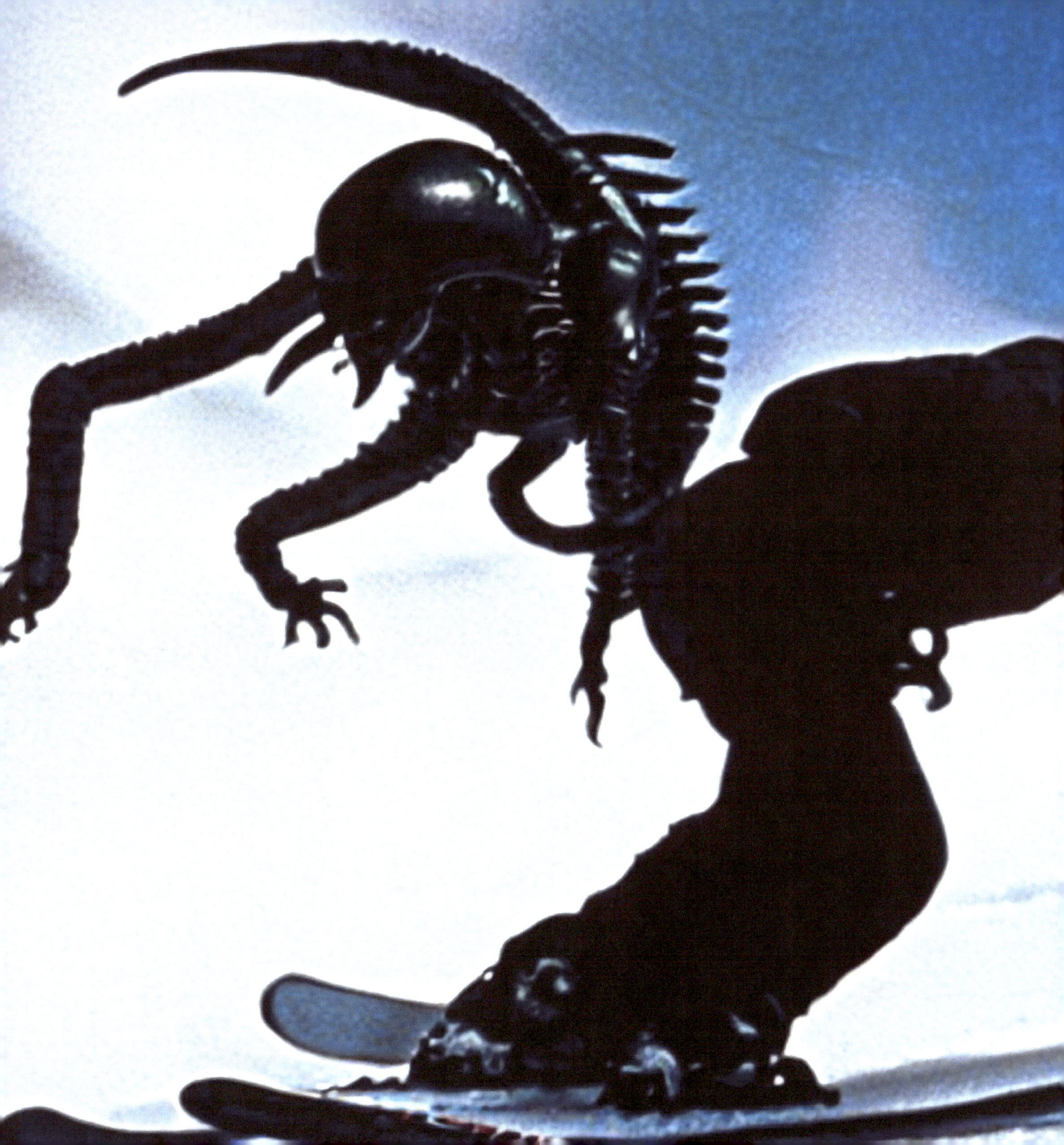

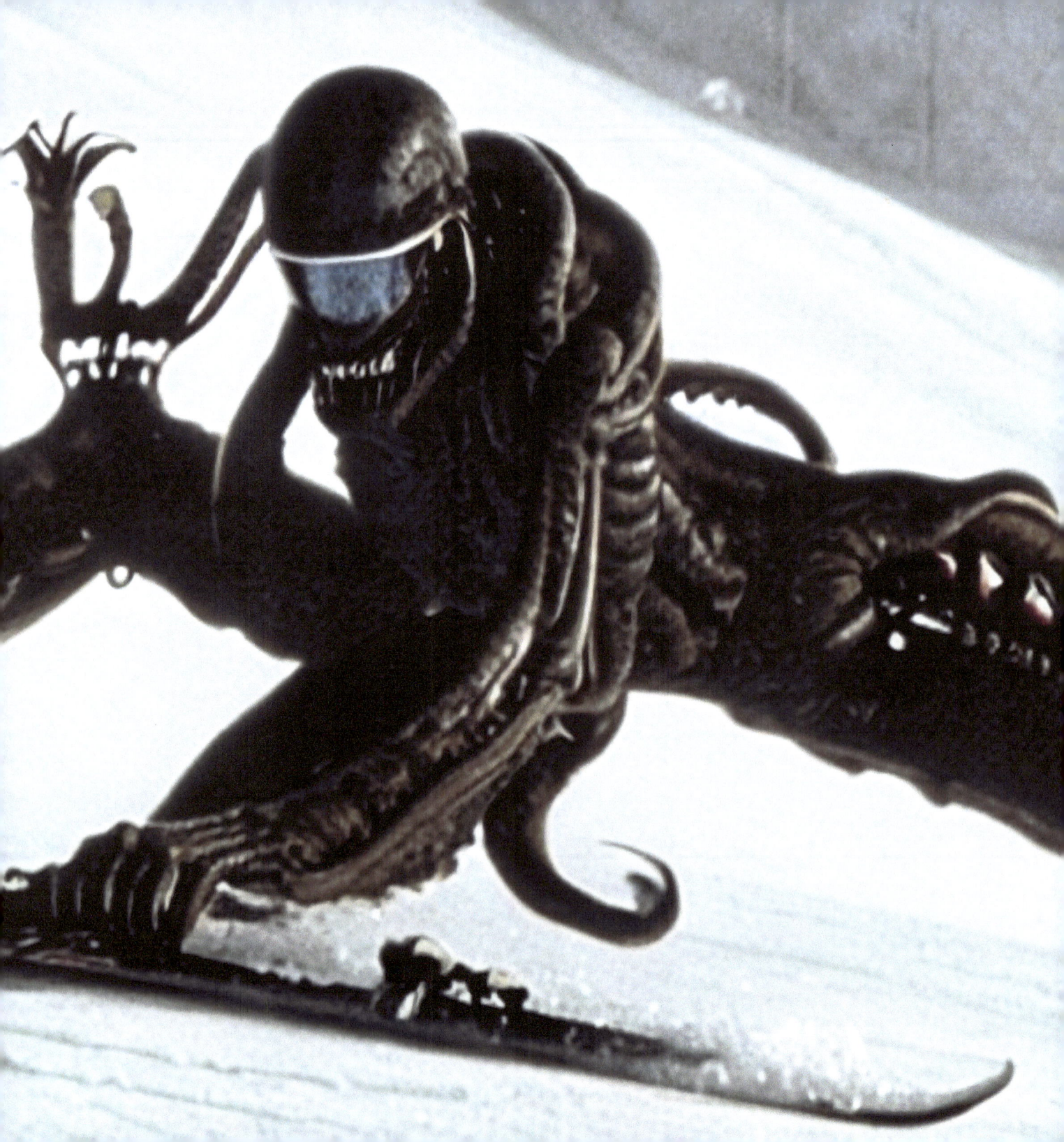

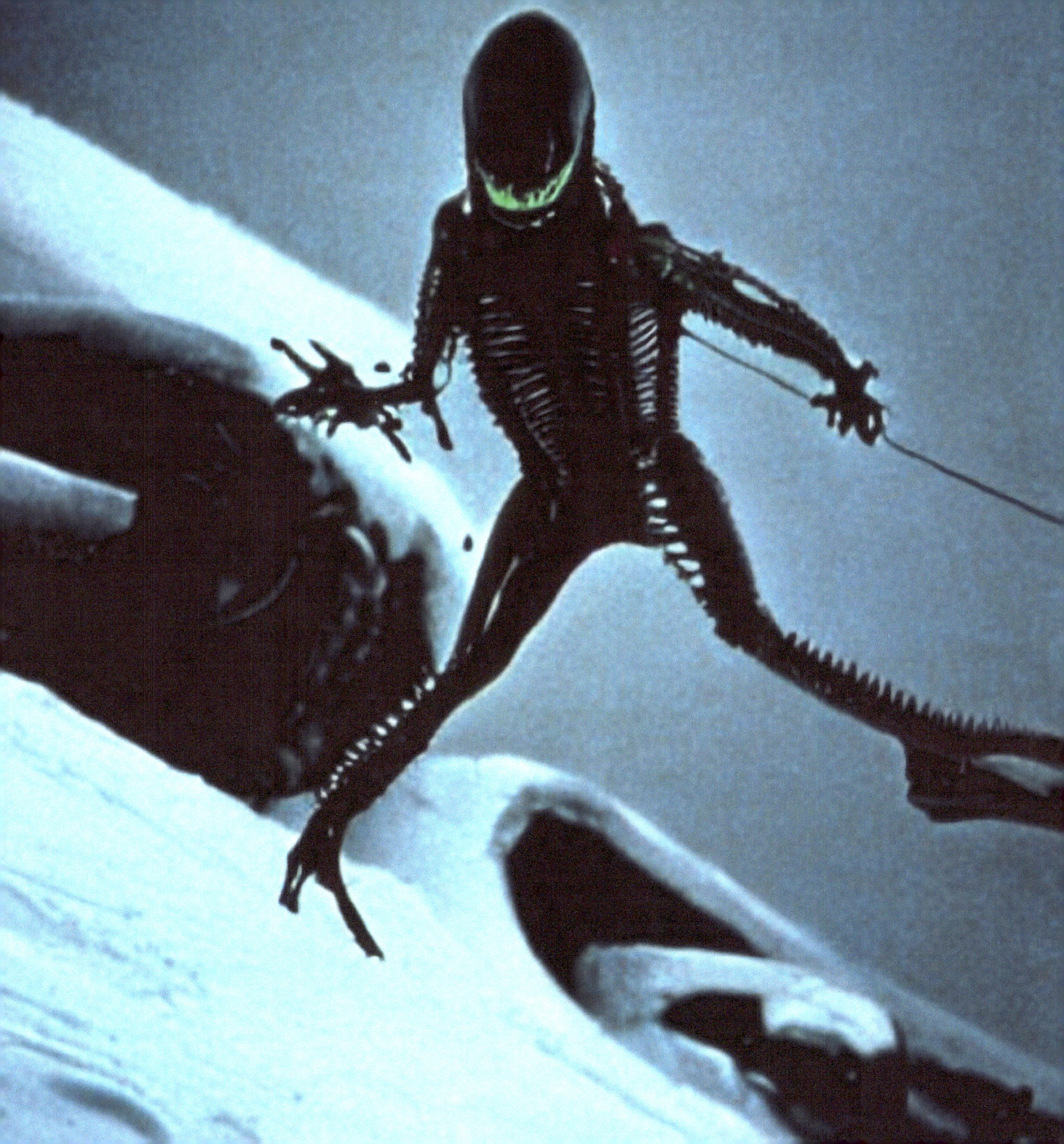

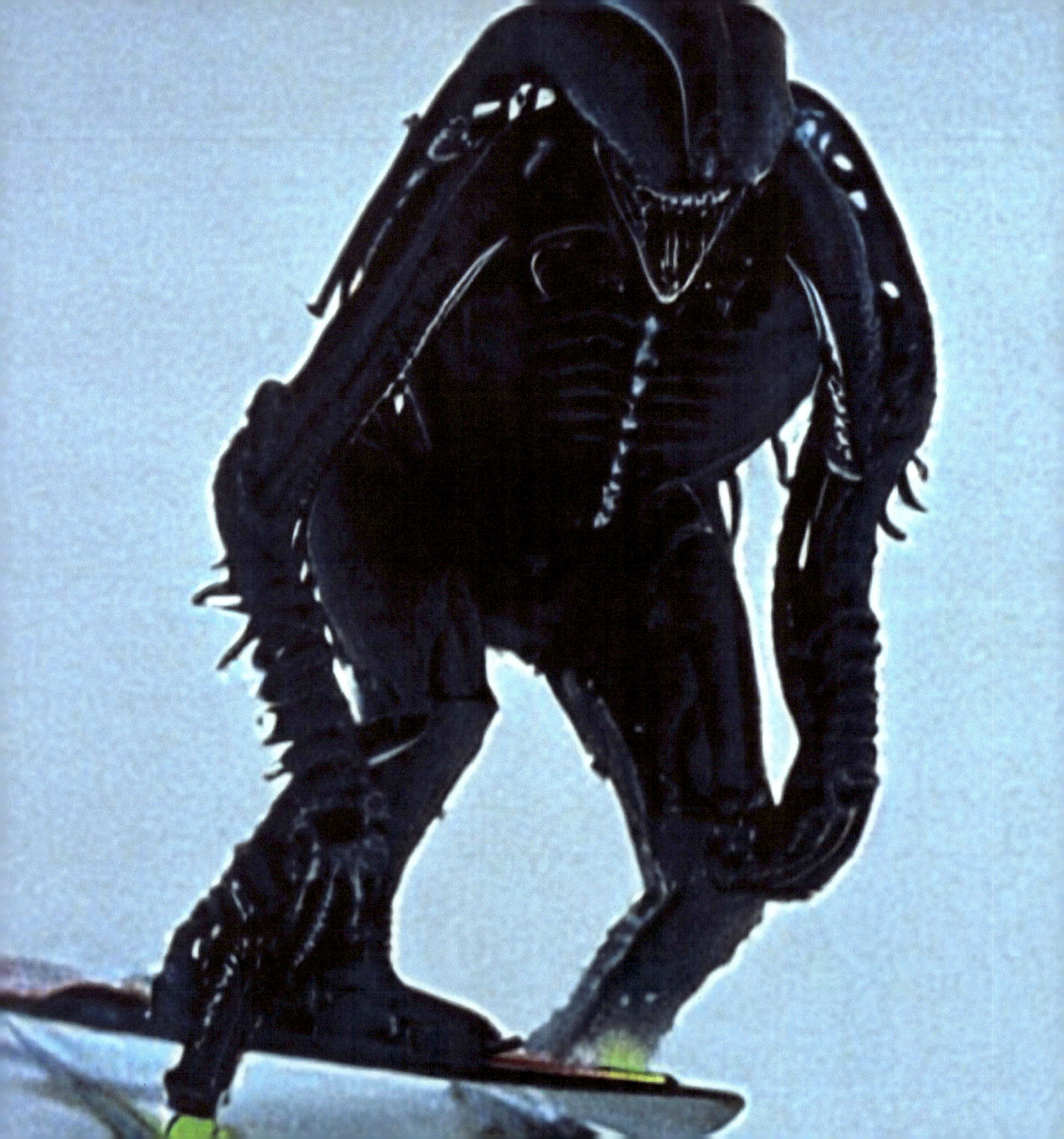

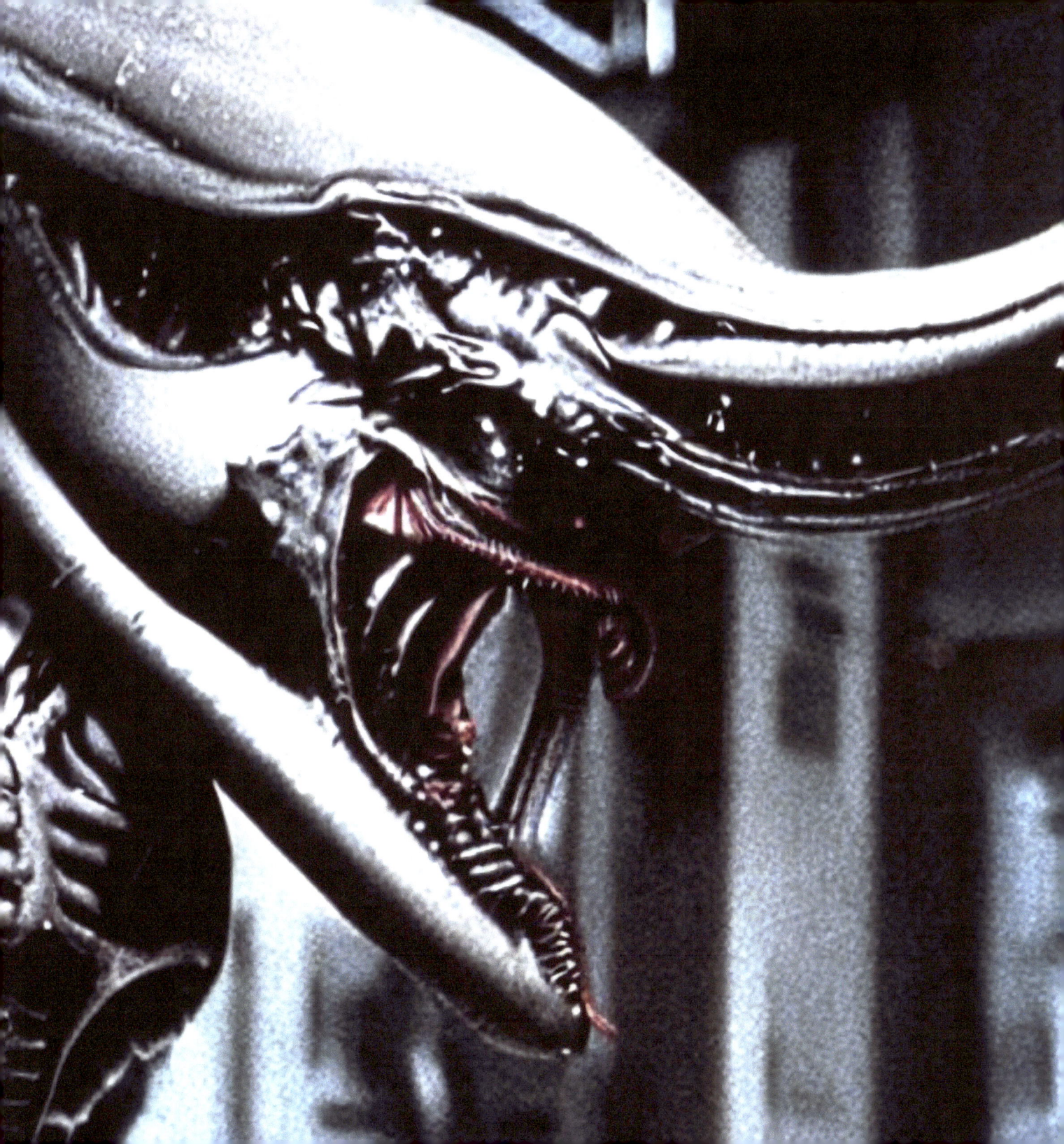

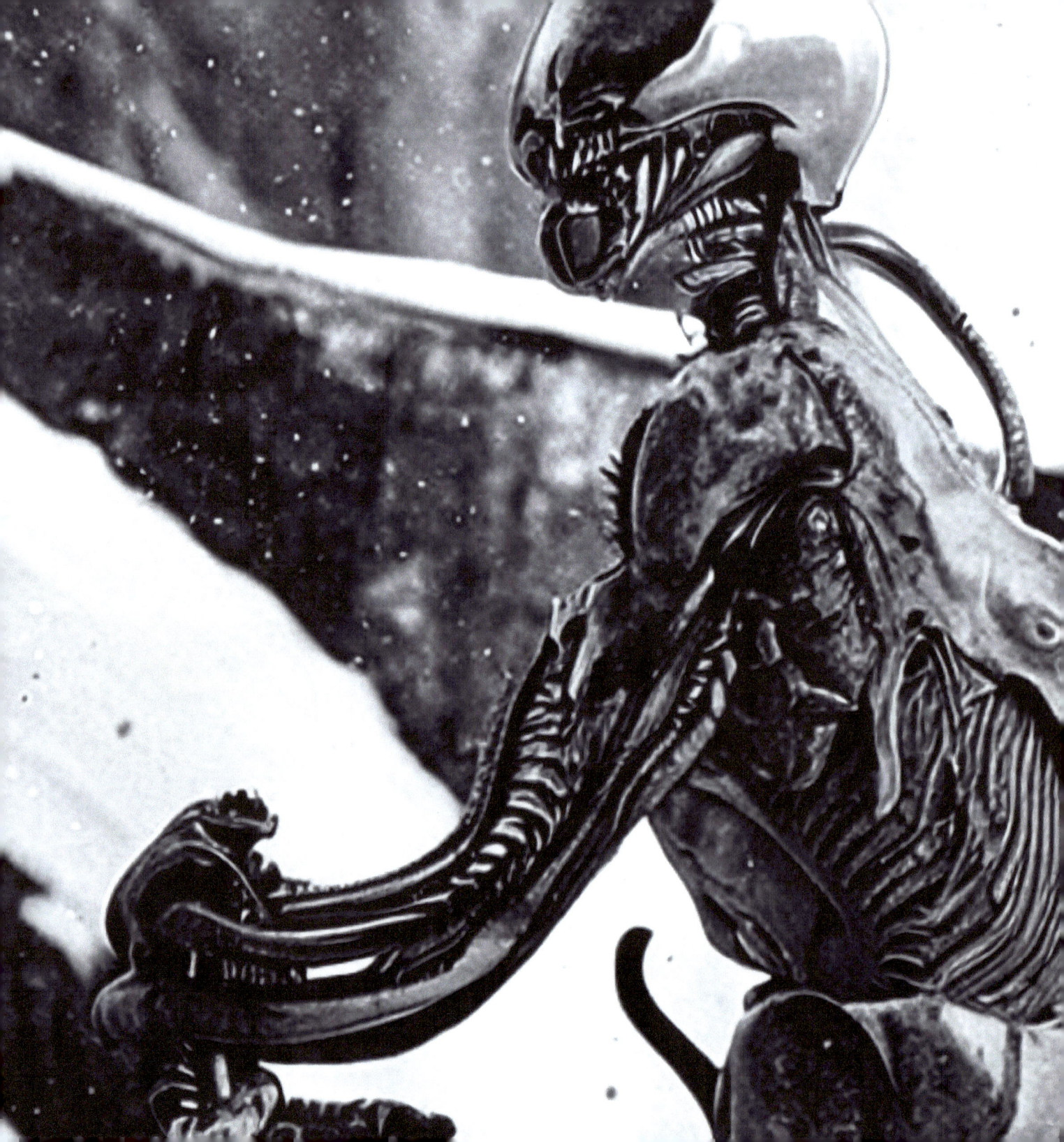

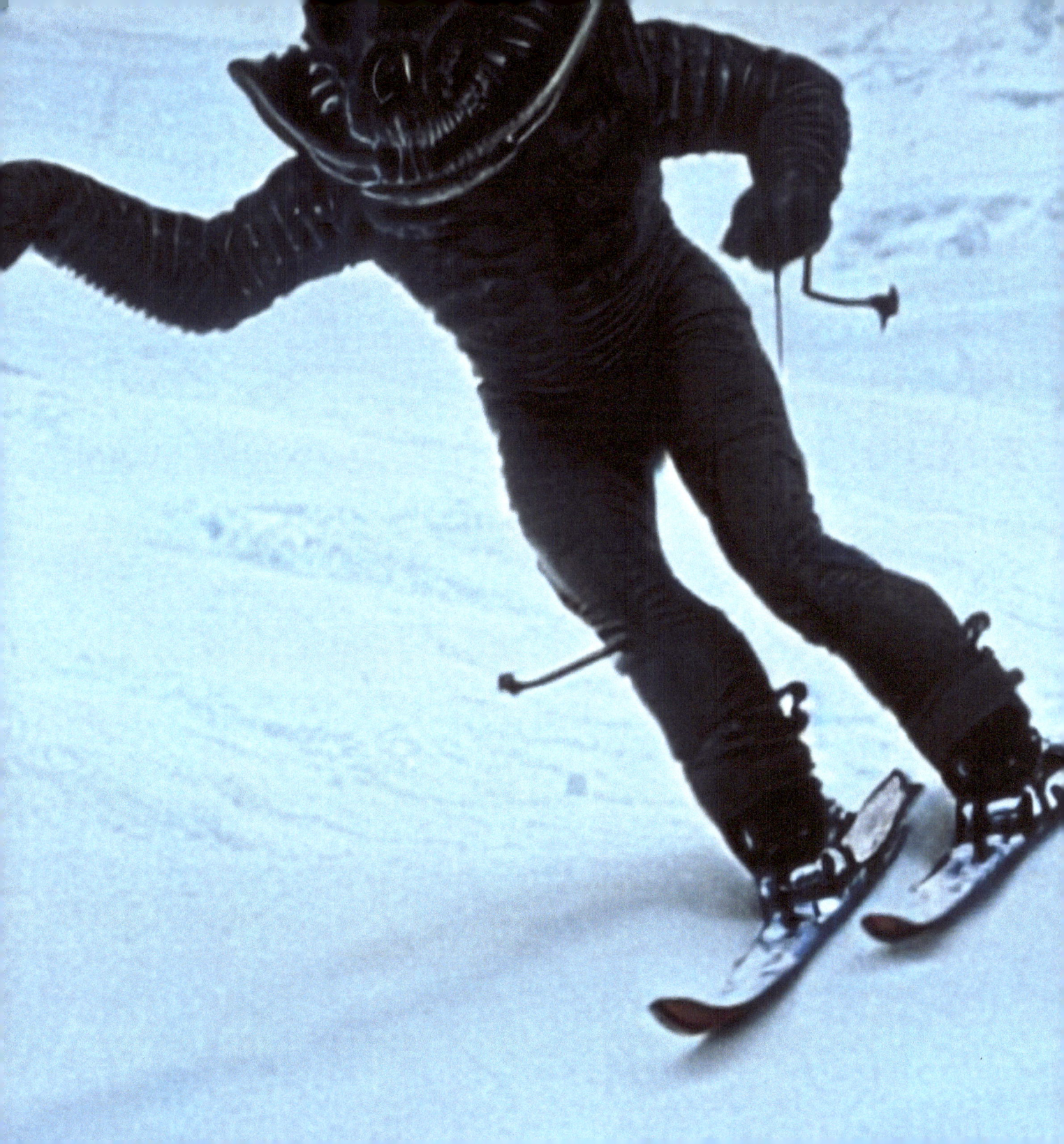

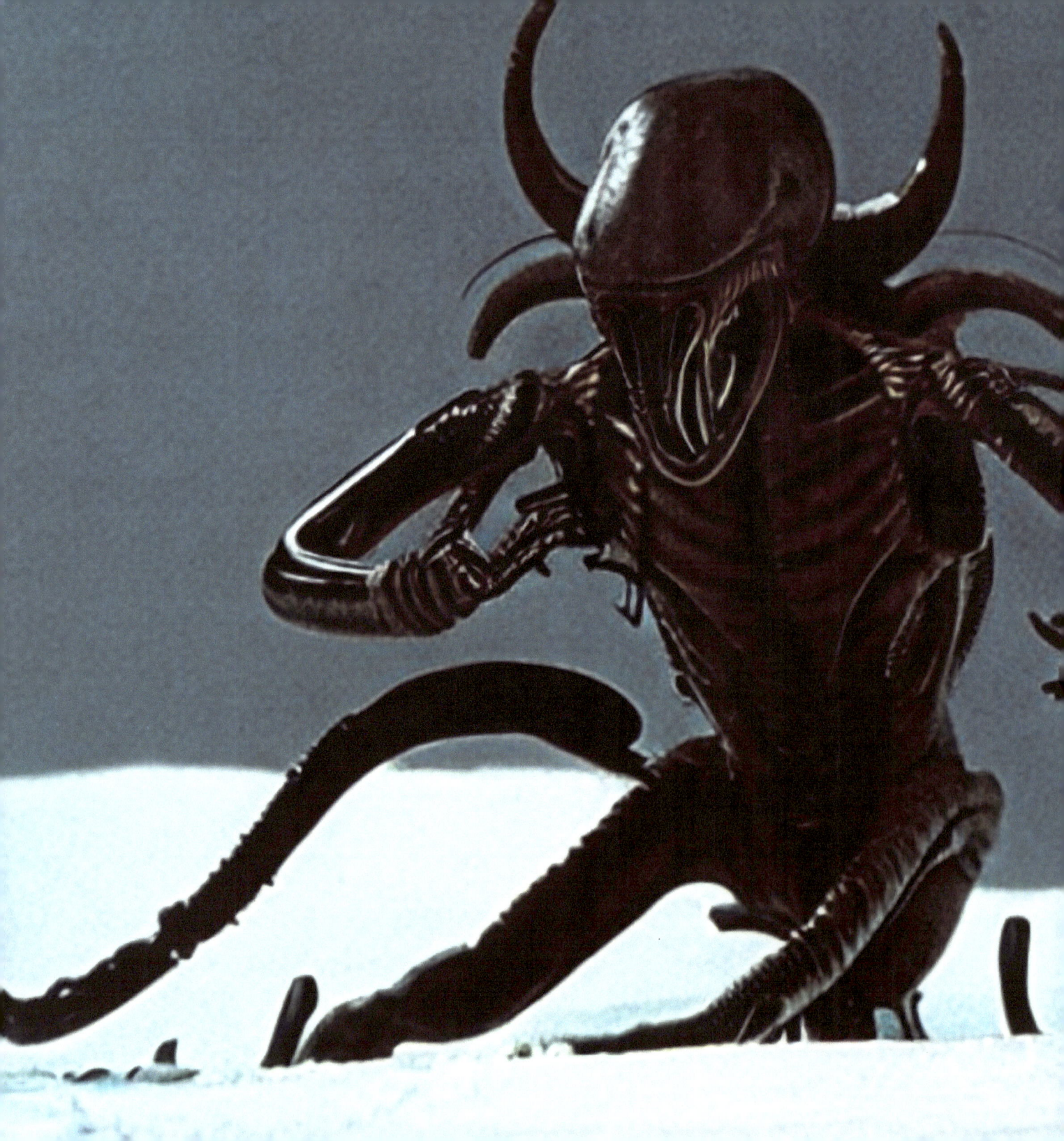

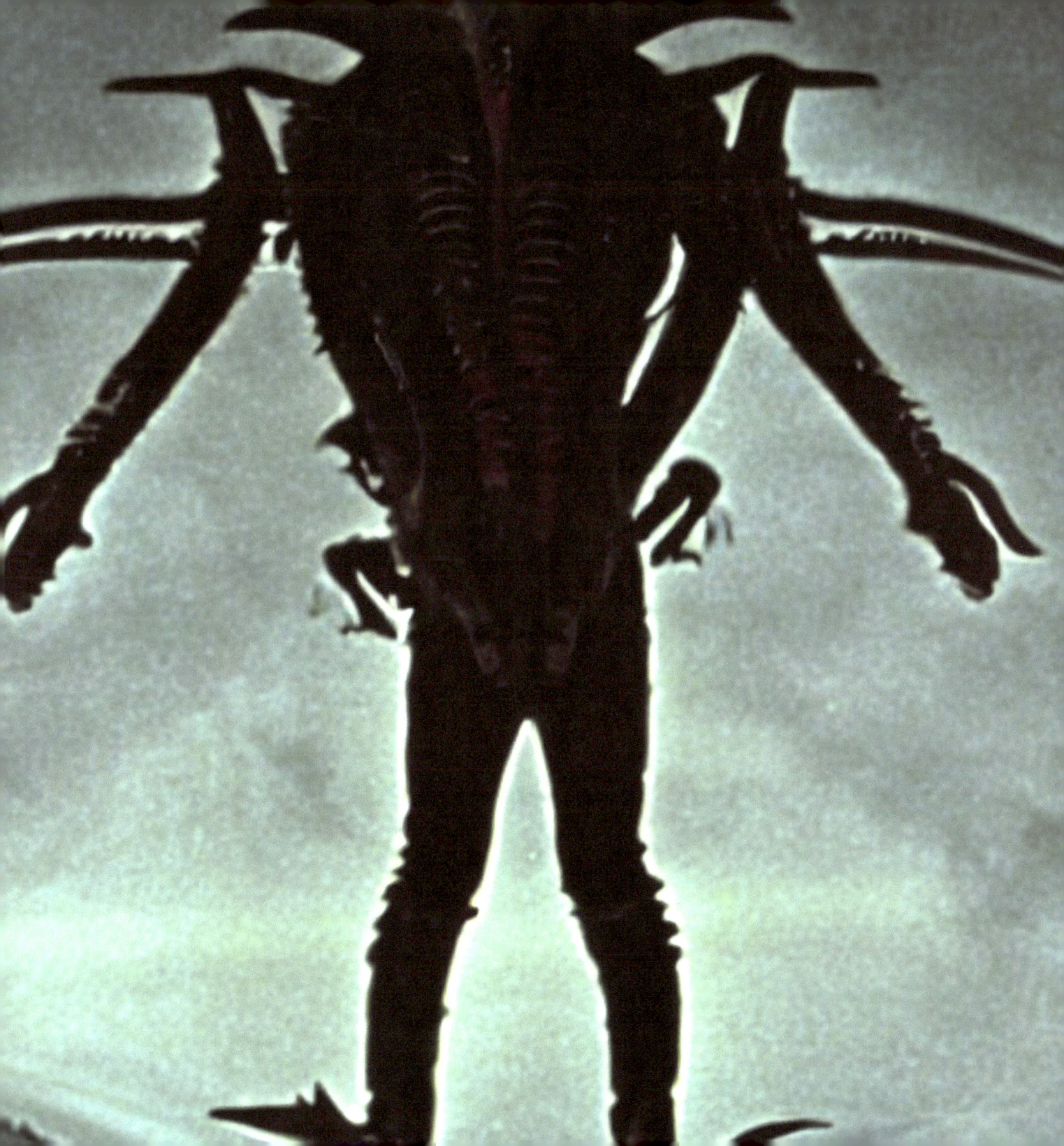

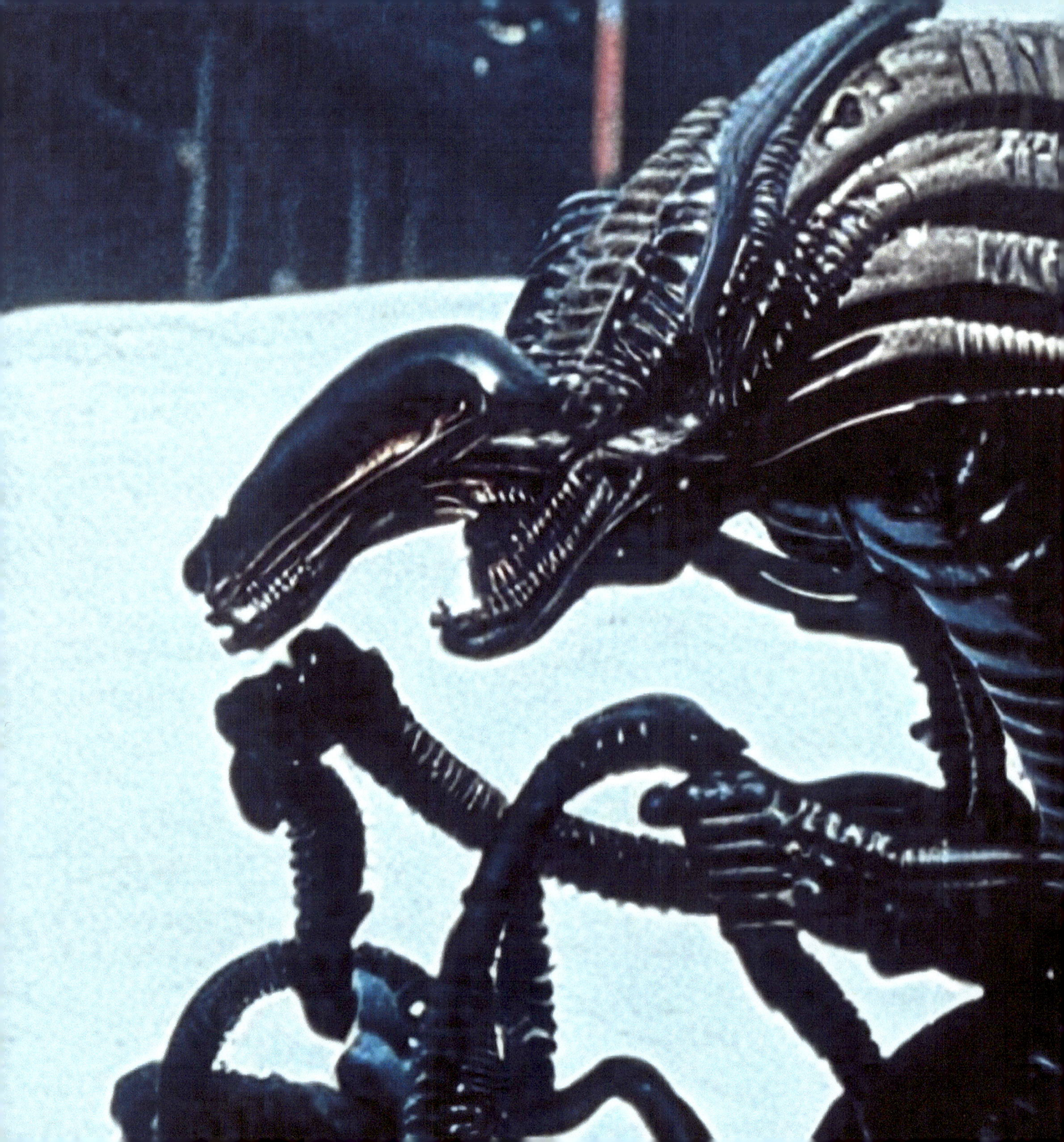

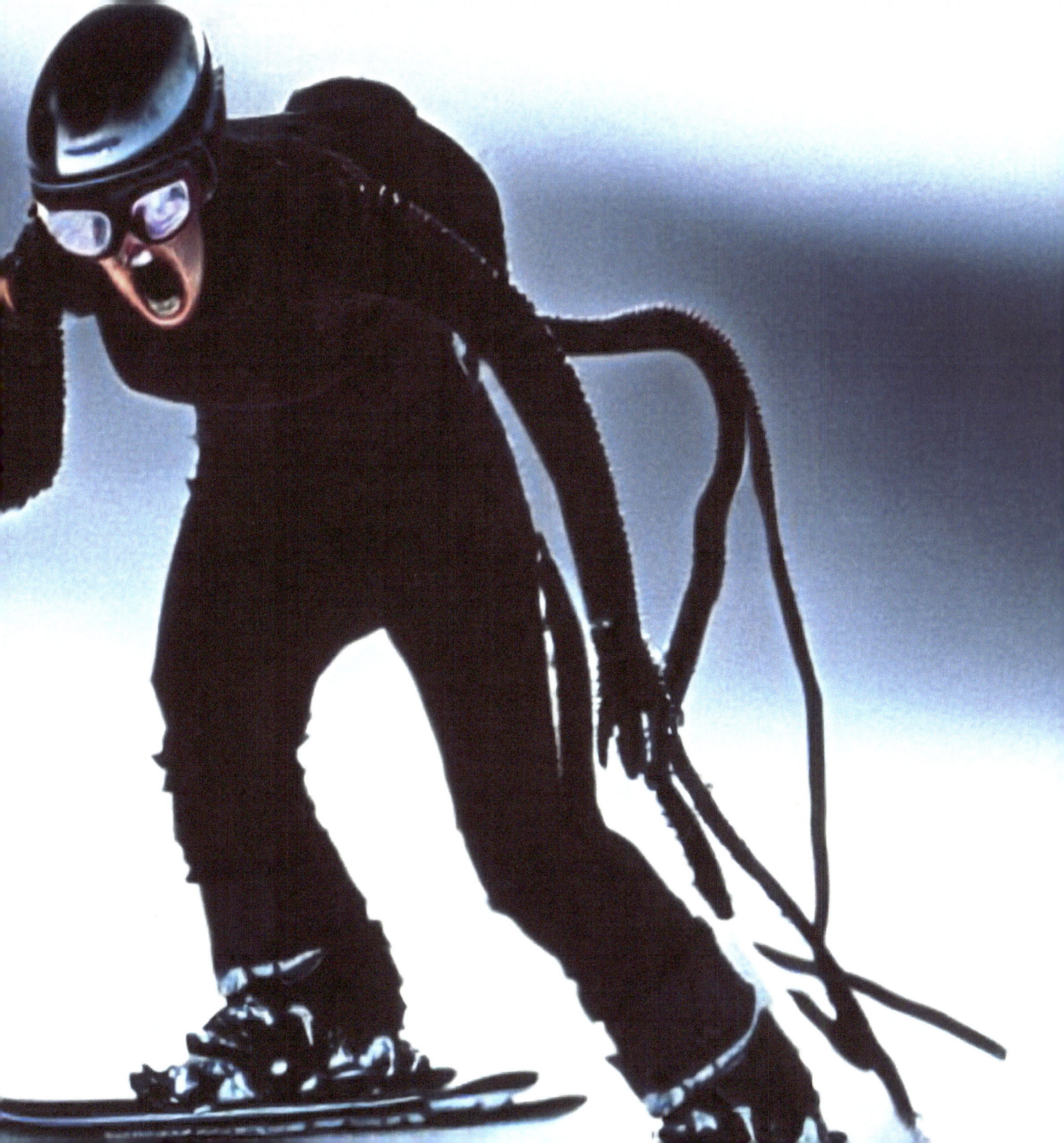

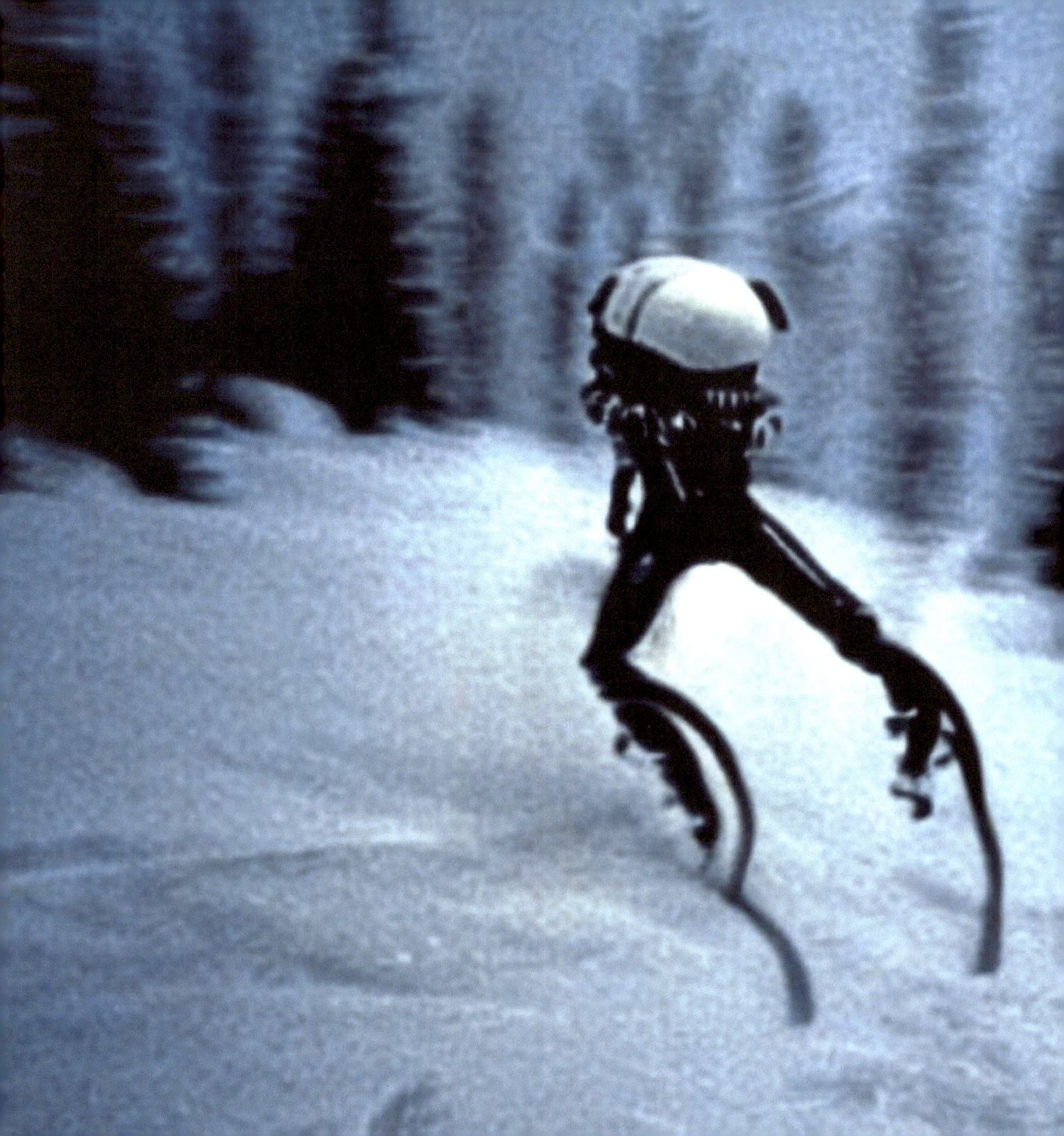

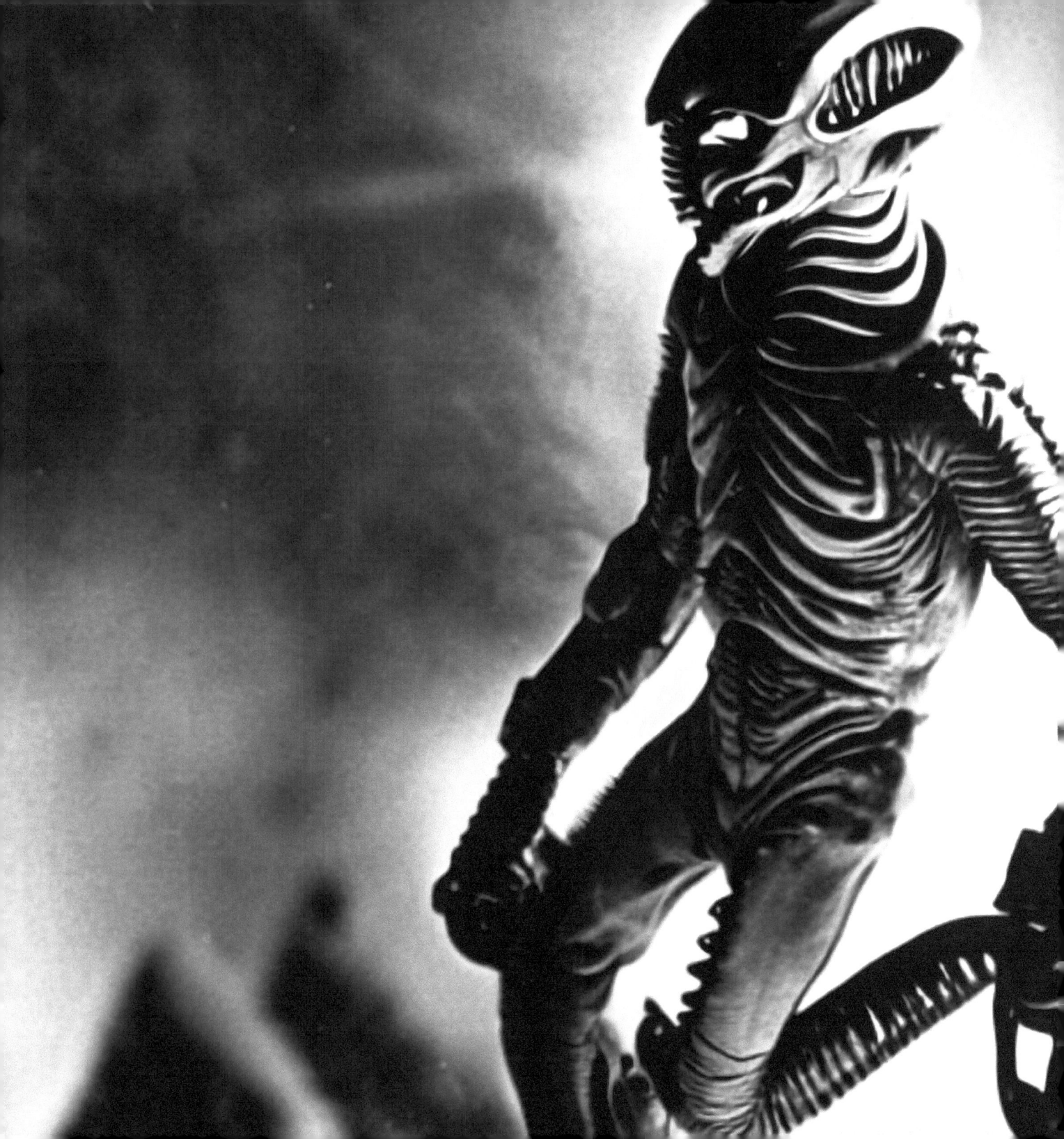

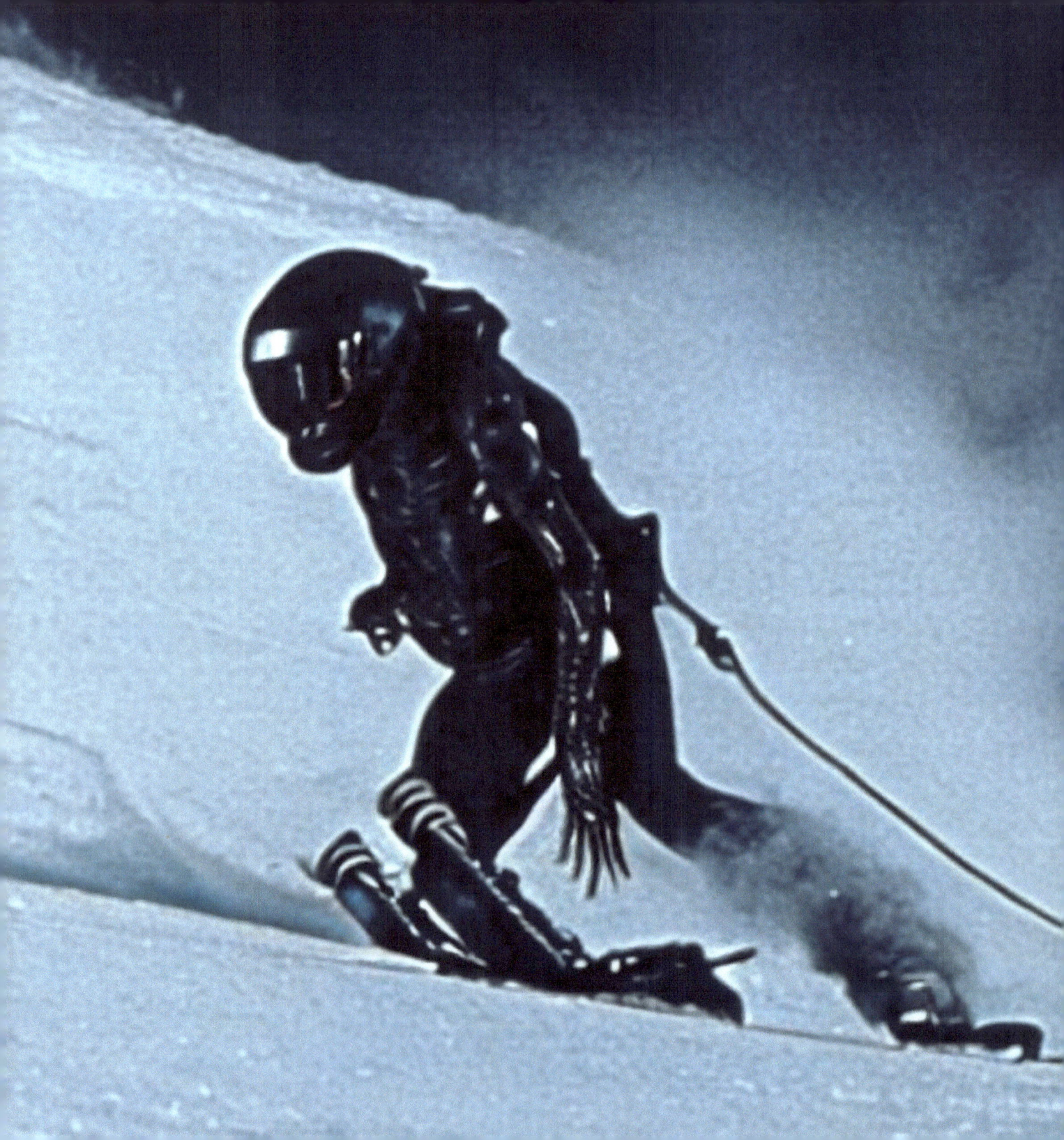

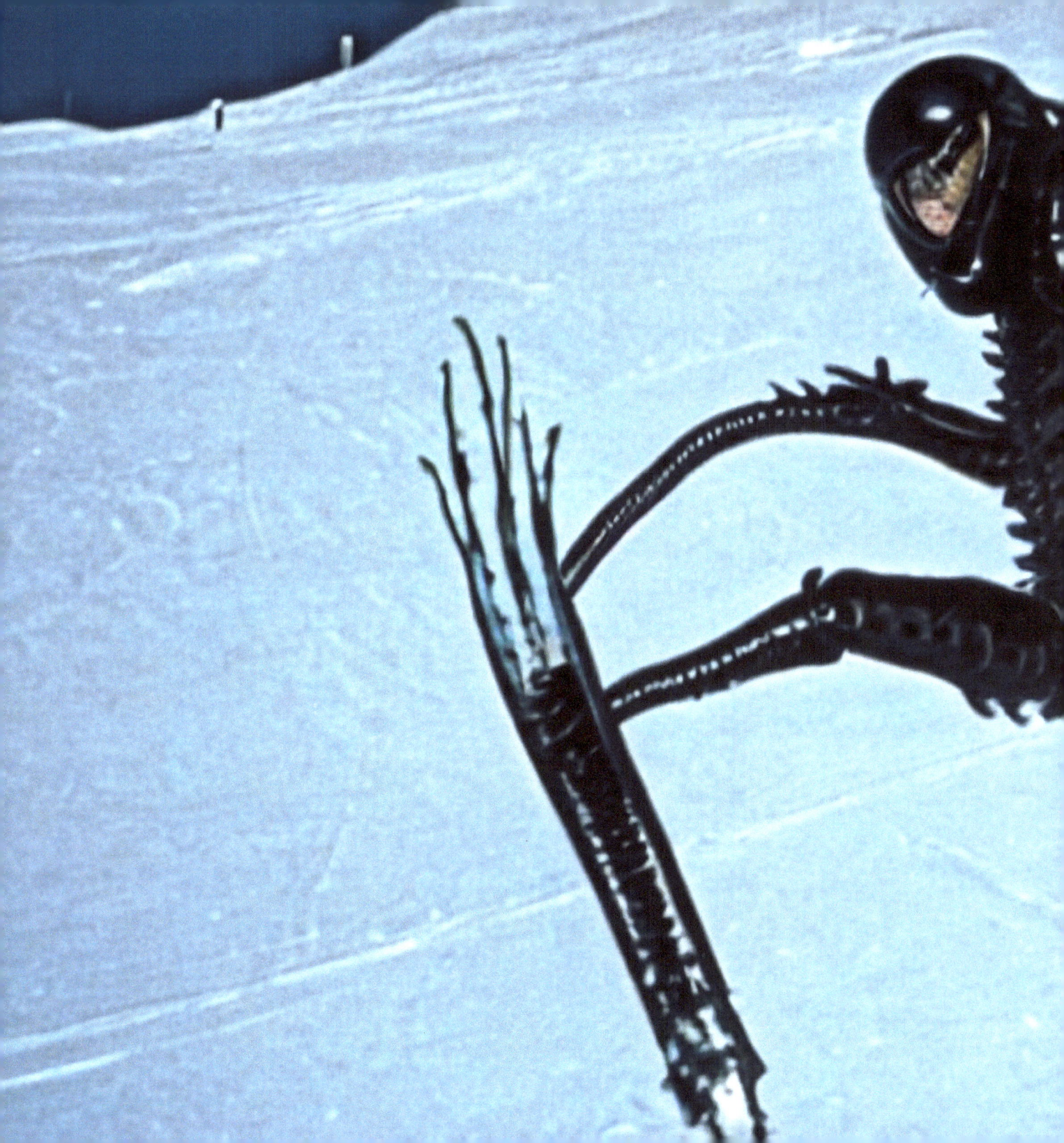

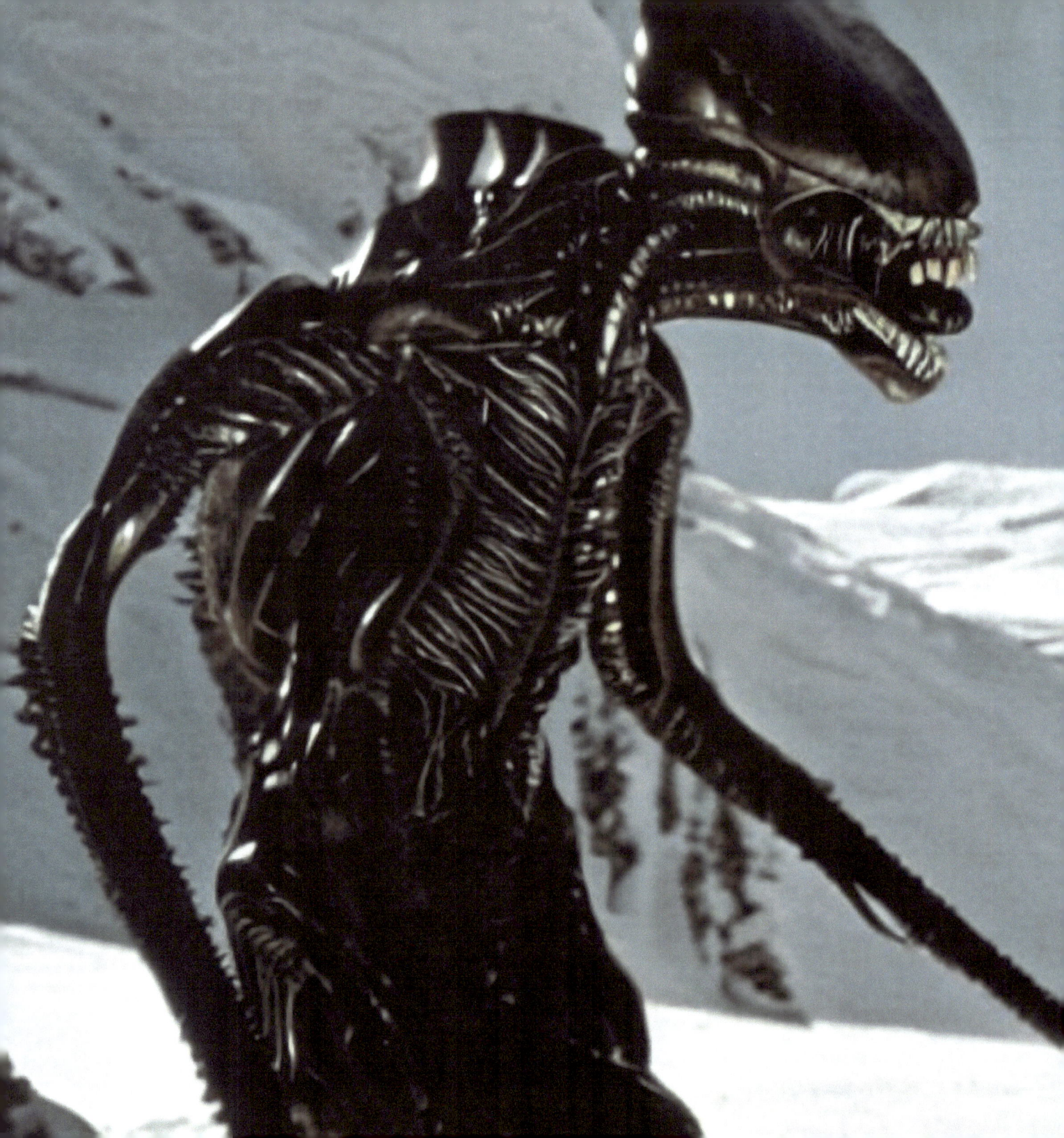

www.ingramcontent.com/pod-product-compliance
Lightning Source LLC
Chambersburg PA
CBHW040417220526
45473CB00004B/1268